My Year of Chevy:

One Guy's Journey Through the Filmography of Chevy Chase

by
Mike
McGranaghan

ISBN 978-1-304-16206-9

Cover illustration by Mike Bennett

Table of Contents

Special thanks to Stephen Kessler for his generosity and insight.

This book is dedicated to Stephanie and Logan, the best family a guy could ask for.

And to Chevy. Thanks for the many laughs.

Introduction

I think Chevy Chase is the world's funniest human being. This is not to say that he always does funny things. I mean, the man *has* had his share of bombs. Yet even when working with substandard material, he rarely fails to make me laugh.

Part of the reason why I am such a fan is that he shaped my view of comedy. When I was a kid, I absorbed all the usual pieces of kiddie entertainment, and "comedy" to me meant Bob Hope specials, Flip Wilson in a dress, and reruns of *The Brady Bunch*. One Sunday morning in 1975, my family was sitting around the breakfast table. (I was seven.) My father began excitedly telling my mother and me about a late night comedy show he'd watched the night before. That, of course, was *Saturday Night Live*. He particularly raved about this performer named Chevy Chase, who did a pratfall and parodied the news. I was intrigued by this person who was supposedly so funny.

A couple years later, I saw Chevy's starring film debut, *Foul Play*, on cable. He was funny and charismatic. I was hooked. Around this same time, NBC started running *SNL* reruns in prime time. I absorbed them. Chevy was only on for a season, but his episodes were, and still are, my favorites.

From then on, I'd rent his latest movies on VHS, catch them on HBO, see them in theaters (if I was allowed), and have repeating viewings of his *SNL* episodes whenever they aired. The "kiddie" comedies of years past no longer appealed to me, nor did the fish-in-a-barrel jokes of Bob Hope. I was into this new kind of humor. Chevy could be edgy and silly simultaneously. He could play dumb while still radiating a fierce intelligence. There was often a political and social edge to his humor. It was fascinating to my young, comedy-obsessed mind. Whenever he had a new project, whether it was a TV comedy special or a new film, I didn't miss it.

Chevy's big screen career had the usual ups and downs. For every *National Lampoon's Vacation*, there was a *Nothing But Trouble*. Eventually, there were too many *Nothing But Trouble*s in a row, and Chevy largely disappeared. Oh, he still worked – it was just bit parts in generic, low-rent crap like *Snow Day* or unreleased comedies. I longed for him to make a comeback. And then he did. A generation of filmmakers grew up, as I did, loving his unique comic stylings. They began to hire him for interesting projects, like *Ellie Parker* and *Orange County*. He did television work, appearing on *Brothers & Sisters* and *Chuck*, before finding his best role in years, as Pierce Hawthorne on the NBC series *Community*. It finally happened: Chevy Chase was cool again.

So why write a book about his movies? Simple: they mean something to me. Good, bad, or indifferent, I am always grateful for the chance to see Chevy do his thing. Yes, I'd rather see him in a first-rate film than a hunk of junk, but the simple truth is that *he* makes me laugh, no matter what. There's just something about him. A related, secondary reason is that Chevy's hits and misses have been far more dramatic than those of just about any other actor out there. He's made movies that are now regarded as classics, and he's made bombs that are still used as punchlines. Tracking the career arc of an actor, film by film, seemed like it could be interesting and enlightening. He seemed like just the right subject.

There are some of Chevy's flicks that I've seen a dozen times and know by heart (*Fletch* being one of them). Many others I hadn't seen in several years, or even decades. A couple of the most recent I'd never seen at all. I wondered what I would learn about his career if I consumed his filmography in a short period of time. With this goal in mind, I set out to re-watch and perform a critical analysis of every single picture he had ever been involved with, to see what memories they stirred, to see if the bad ones are as bad as I remember, and to see if any of the non-hits reveal themselves to be unsung winners. And I gave myself twelve months to do it. This was to be my Year of Chevy.

What you are about to read is the product of that undertaking, which was indeed enlightening. I hope you enjoy it.

The Groove Tube

Chevy's first big screen appearance was in 1974's *The Groove Tube*, a precursor to the likes of *SCTV* and other shows that poked fun at television. Written and directed by Ken Shapiro (who would re-team with Chevy years later on *Modern Problems*), the film is a series of sketches that represent the programming of a fictional TV station called Channel One. The sketches run the gamut from parodies of kids' programs (a clown reads erotic literature), to a newscast, to a cooking show, to a Wide World of Sports spoof. Fake commercials are interspersed throughout.

If ever a movie was the product of its era, this one is it. I suspect *The Groove Tube* might have been funny had it been seen in 1974 – and had the audience been high as a kite. The comedy is definitely of the stoner variety. Heck, the fake TV station may as well have been called WTHC. That's how pot-centric the humor is. Shapiro's jabs at TV seem mild by today's standards, and the individual skits are both endless and unimaginatively shot. Consider "Channel One's Wild World of Sports," in which two commentators narrate something called the International Sex Games, providing graphic descriptions of what a nude couple is doing in bed. The joke of the piece is that the picture cuts out during the most graphic moments, only to be replaced by a "Please Stand By" card. That card is visible for several minutes during the sketch. While there is some inherent humor in an audience not being able to see the insane things the commentators are talking about, the concept is funny for maybe a minute, tops.

After five or six minutes, you can't help but feel aggravated about watching a static shot of three words against a blue background. Most of the bits end up in this same state of wearing out their welcome.

Chevy's total screen time totals about three minutes. His first appearance is the most unusual. He stars in a fake vitamin commercial, extolling the virtues of the vitamins he bought for his wife, which have made her more energetic and lively. Meanwhile, the actress playing his wife strips naked and hops into bed with him. The payoff is Chevy delivering the commercial's tag line while she performs a sex act on him beneath the covers. Wow, those are some vitamins, huh? Every married couple needs at least one partner who takes those!

What makes this sketch notable is that Chevy's voice has clearly been dubbed by someone who sounds nothing like him. I mean, they could have dubbed him with Fran Drescher and it would have been a better match. Why this was done, I cannot say. In 1974, before he was a household name, it's doubtful anyone noticed. Seeing the movie today, it's blatant. The thing is, Chevy has a very distinctive comic delivery – one that mixes sarcasm and sincerity in almost equal measure. The person who dubbed his voice has a flat tone that robs the material of any punch. Apparently, the intention was to mimic the style of an authoritative-yet-dull announcer; but since anyone who ever watched *Saturday Night Live* knows Chevy did this sort of thing quite effectively in that show's phony ads, the failure to let him do it in *The Groove Tube* is confounding. Maybe Ken Shapiro could not see what *SNL* producer Lorne Michaels clearly did, a year later.

The next time we see Chevy, we only see his fingers. In a parody of those "let your fingers do the talking" phone book ads of the era, two sets of fingers begin twisting themselves into clearly sexual positions. I think you can understand why being high might help make the material seem funny. Fingers engaging in intercourse is really only hysterical if you're tripping balls. Nonetheless, this skit represents the first instance of Chevy's patented "hand comedy," which we will discuss in more detail later on.

After the fingers, it takes the better part of 45 minutes for Chevy to show up again. As part of a barbershop duet (not a quartet, but a duet), he sings "I'm Looking Over a Four Leaf Clover" while another actor slaps his head like a drum. At the end of the song, the other man slaps Chevy so hard that he falls over and out of the frame.

The Groove Tube may have helped put Chevy on the map, but it didn't really let him do much of anything. In one sketch, he's dubbed. In another, we only see his fingers. In the third, he merely sings and is, more or less, the straight man. Given his immense comic gifts, it's bizarre that his talents are so vastly underused.

The other prominent note is that *The Groove Tube* features an extended spoof of the evening news, not at all unlike the Weekend Update bit that Chevy established on *SNL* a year later. The newscast, which features reporters with names such as Thurthon Thithtertinton, ends with the anchor signing off with the catchphrase, "Good night, and have a pleasant tomorrow." Chevy, of course, used that phrase weekly as he ended his own faux newscast. If nothing else, at least the movie provided a little something to comedy culture.

Now regarded as something of a cult classic, *The Groove Tube* is an artifact of a time when spoofing TV was new and daring. And it's a badly dated artifact, at that.

Foul Play

After an extremely successful year on *Saturday Night Live*, Chevy famously left the show to pursue a career in movies. (He's also stated that he headed for California to be with a woman.) His first post-stardom foray into film came in the form of 1978's *Foul Play*. Largely conceived as a vehicle for Goldie Hawn, the picture is the story of Gloria Mundy, a mild-mannered librarian who, in what she thinks is an act of kindness, picks up a stranded motorist. Unbeknownst to her, the man is being chased by a bunch of nefarious figures. He discreetly slips a roll of film into a cigarette pack and drops it into Gloria's purse. Later, he shows up at her apartment wounded, and tells her to "beware of the dwarf" before keeling over.

A day later, Gloria is attacked by a mysterious albino who is looking for the film roll. She eludes him by ducking into a bar and asking to go home with Stanley Tibbets (Dudley Moore), an innocent-looking man sitting alone. Stanley thinks he's getting lucky and proudly displays the inner workings of his bachelor pad, which include a mirrorball above the bed, a closet full of sex toys, and a stereo that pumps out Bee Gees tunes. Once she's convinced that she's given the albino the slip, Gloria apologizes to Stanley for the misunderstanding and returns home, where she is once again attacked, this time by a man with a scar.

Chevy plays Tony Carlson, the police detective who arrives on the scene after this attack. Gloria tries to convince him of all the unusual occurrences she's been through. Tony is skeptical, but also attracted to the young woman. He almost humors her by conducting an investigation. Some clues come together, though, and Tony figures out that Gloria has gotten stuck in the middle of a conspiracy to assassinate the Pope. The movie ends with a shootout at the Opera House, where Tony foils the assassination plot and ends up kissing Gloria onstage, while Stanley stands in the orchestra pit, conducting the musicians.

Foul Play is a notable entry in the Chevy Chase canon because it represents one of the few times he had demonstrable chemistry with a female co-star. (Beverly D'Angelo in the *Vacation* pictures being the other most notable example.) One need look no further than a long, sustained shot in which Gloria and Tony start to kiss. Their lips rest mere millimeters apart, but for the longest time, they simply make flirtatious comments to one another; it's almost like a contest to see who will break first. Finally, they do, and it's a surprisingly magical kiss.

The two stars prove to be a winning combination. Hawn does a variation on her trademark ditzy routine, while Chevy somehow mixes suaveness with a hint of being sardonic. The two play off each other well, finding a comic rhythm that suits them both. Over the years, Chevy has stated in interviews that he and Hawn became close friends, which may, in part, account for their successful pairing. In contrast, it's been widely reported that he didn't like Demi Moore, and look at how non-existent their chemistry is in *Nothing But Trouble*.

The film represented a unique moment for Chevy. The role of Tony Carlson requires an almost old-fashioned sense of Leading Man charisma. Some critics even compared him favorably to Cary Grant in this role. Chevy does manage to work in a few slapstick moments – he knocks over some drinks at a bar, and later pratfalls into the ocean – but for the most part, he exudes a suaveness that rarely, if ever, seemed to interest him again. Interestingly, he undersells most of his comic lines. Rather than playing them as obvious jokes, Chevy restrains himself, making them part of the character's natural charm. Tony Carlson remains one of his best, most committed roles. Chevy was nominated for a Golden Globe in the Best Actor – Motion Picture

Musical or Comedy category, but lost to Warren Beatty in
Heaven Can Wait.

Foul Play holds up pretty well. It's kind of an odd film
when you think about it; the sweetly quirky romantic-comedy
moments sometimes clash with the more outrageous comic-
thriller moments. There are fast-paced dialogue scenes which
have an old-fashioned screwball-romance feel bumping up
against broad comedy sequences that involve sex toys and
Japanese tourists unwittingly stuck in a car chase. Nevertheless,
the laughs come pretty consistently, and the Chevy/Goldie
chemistry provides the movie with enough heart to ground the
more out-there bits. Dudley Moore's supporting performance is
also a vital asset, as he perfectly plays a sex fiend who knows
how to dress up in a nerd's clothes. Chevy is actually the one who
lobbied for Moore to get the role, which was then tailored to his
comedic strengths. The plot is excessively far-fetched, which
becomes apparent in the third act, when one villainous character
stops to over-explain the reasons behind the assassination
attempt. The light pace provided by director Colin Higgins
prevents that from becoming a fatal flaw, though. Mostly, *Foul
Play* is just a lot of fun, even if all the great individual bits don't
quite add up to a great whole.

Interesting Trivia:

The name of Hawn's character, Gloria Mundy, derives from the
Latin phrase *sic transit gloria mundi*, which means "thus passes
the glory of the world." It was historically used in papal
coronation ceremonies, which is fitting, given *Foul Play*'s central
plot device.

Foul Play was spun off into a short-lived TV series, with
Deborah Raffin and Barry Bostwick filling in for Hawn and
Chevy.

Oh! Heavenly Dog

In the history of bad ideas, few have been as bad as *Oh! Heavenly Dog*, a motion picture that nearly defies description. Even today, it provides a go-to punchline for anyone who wants to reference a notoriously bad movie. The execution is terrible, for sure, but the concept was dubious to begin with. It's almost impossible to imagine a good movie being made from this premise – or at least a good PG-rated family film. (It might work as an R-rated adult comedy.) In his original review, Roger Ebert said, "every scene in the movie is directed at the same deadening crawl, most of the dialogue is delivered in a dispirited monotone, and the solution, when it comes, is shatteringly uninteresting." Truer words may never have been written.

Dog opens with Chevy playing Benjamin Browning, an American private investigator working in rainy London. He literally bumps into a beautiful young writer named Jackie (Jane Seymour) and makes a tentative date to see her again. Before they can rendezvous, Browning is murdered in the course of investigating a case and discovering a dead body. He goes to Heaven, which turns out to be a bureaucratic hell, and is told that he must return to Earth to solve his own murder. There is a hitch: since he can't go back in his own body, he must return in another one. And the body they give him belongs to a dog, played by 70s/80s kids' movie icon Benji.

Plopped back into London, Browning sneaks into various locations looking for clues. His tactics are largely an excuse to show off Benji the dog's abilities: he dials a phone, flips the pages of a desk calendar, etc. The story's villain, played by Omar Sharif, figures out that the pooch is on to him and plots to have him killed. At one point, Browning is given the opportunity to leave Earth and proceed to Heaven once and for all. Knowing that Jackie - who has been investigating the same case for a book she plans to write - will likely be killed too, he opts to remain a dog forever so that he can finish his work and prevent her from meeting harm. Using his wits, he does indeed expose the conspiracy that led to two murders, including his own. As soon as the guilty party is exposed, a gun is pulled on the dog. Realizing in this moment that Benji is actually the nice man she had planned to go on a date with, Jackie jumps in front of him, taking the bullet. She is then reincarnated as a stray cat. The movie ends with her and the now-permanently canine Browning walking off into the sunset.

If a family film centered around a double murder sounds questionable, the rest of *Oh! Heavenly Dog* makes sure to push the boundaries even further with an abundance of inappropriate humor. After an opening credits sequence set to the Paul McCartney/Wings song "Arrow Through Me," Browning gets in a car with his flamboyant friend Freddie, played by former *Laugh-In* regular Alan Sues. It is implied that Freddie grabs Browning's privates while "reaching for the gear shift." That's right – an offensive gay joke four minutes into a Benji the dog movie. There are plenty more. Later in the film, it is revealed that Freddie has died in an accident and also returned to Earth, although he comes in feline form. Upon being reunited with Browning, he immediately proceeds to look between the dog's legs and then rub himself underneath his old pal.

The non-homophobic jokes are just as out of place. During his initial assessment of life as a dog, Browning says "It's amazing how much bigger everything looks from down here." He then takes a peek at his doggie genitals and adds, "Well, not everything." At one point, the canine Browning nuzzles up to Jackie's breasts in a sexual manner. When she goes to take a bath, he watches her undress, then jumps in the tub with her. One gets the sense that *Oh! Heavenly Dog* may, at one point, have been intended as a comedy for adults, but then somehow retrofitted to accommodate for the box office popularity of Benji.

No matter why it exists, this is a bad film. It's also a bad film for Chevy, and he seems to know it. During the 15 minutes he appears in human form at the beginning, he looks bored and uninterested, often giving his dialogue a flat delivery. After Browning is transformed, all Chevy has to do is provide voiceover for static shots of a dog, but even that seems to hold little appeal. Right before the movie's third act begins, the screenplay paints itself into a corner. Unable to figure out a way for a dog to open the top drawer of a file cabinet, there's a *Deus ex machina* in which Browning is abruptly turned human again by the bureaucratic angel who sent him back in the first place. This leads to what is supposed to be the heart of the story: Browning realizing that he loves Jackie and will gladly sacrifice his own afterlife to protect her. Again, Chevy doesn't seem especially invested in the role, so the moment offers no emotion.

It's hard to say what drew Chevy to sign on for *Oh! Heavenly Dog*. Perhaps he thought that it would be a more grown-up picture than it ended up being. The abundance of foul language, a too-complicated-for-kids-to-follow plot, and bursts of risque humor certainly indicate that it might have been envisioned much differently at one point. A more mature take on the material definitely would have been a better fit. For starters, Browning should have had impulses to do natural dog things: pee on hydrants, lick himself, hump everything in sight, and so on. There's much comedic potential in taking seriously the idea of a man suddenly forced to live as a dog. A funnyman as skilled as Chevy might have shown a little more pep had he been allowed to bring more irreverence to the role, whether on camera or simply through voiceover. It certainly would have made for a picture that's easier to sit through.

In interviews over the years since its release, Chevy has largely disowned *Oh! Heavenly Dog*. He knows it is a terrible film, one that runs an inexplicable 106 minutes. For whatever it's worth, he is not alone. The talents of Seymour and Sharif are also wasted. Only Benji comes off looking good, but that's only because you don't often see a dog use a pencil to dial a telephone.

Any way you cut it, *Oh! Heavenly Dog* is a dog of the cinematic variety.

Caddyshack/Caddyshack II

Caddyshack

The sting of *Oh! Heavenly Dog* didn't last long. That film opened on July 11, 1980. Two short weeks later, Chevy would have another picture in theaters, and it would become one of his most revered classics.

Caddyshack probably shouldn't have worked at all. The screenplay began life as a collection of remembrances from director Harold Ramis and actor Brian Doyle-Murray, both of whom worked as caddies when they were adolescents. Together with co-writer Doug Kenney, they fashioned what was essentially a coming-of-age comedy in which a young man named Danny (eventually played by Michael O'Keefe) found his direction in life after spending a summer working at an elite country club. But with the addition of Chevy, Bill Murray, and Rodney Dangerfield – all of whom improvised heavily – *Caddyshack* became something else altogether. Somehow, the picture worked magnificently, despite the shift in direction.

The '80s had a sub-genre of big screen comedy, generally derived from the National Lampoon and *Saturday Night Live* comedians, that became known as the "slobs vs. snobs" movie. Popularized by *Animal House*, films in this sub-genre tended to focus on a lovably ragtag group of friends/associates who used their wits to humiliate and outsmart whatever establishment they found themselves in the midst of (the army in *Stripes*, law enforcement in *The Blues Brothers*, etc). *Caddyshack* is the epitome of "slobs vs. snobs." Set at a posh country club with a noticeably snooty membership, it casts beloved comedians as the heroes who, through their wise-assery, make the story's more uptight, prejudicial, prim-and-proper characters look like complete buffoons. Despite what some people believe, *Caddyshack* is not about golf, it's about bigotry.

The story begins with teenager Danny Noonan getting a lecture from his father, who pushes him to work more hours as a caddy at Bushwood Country Club so that he can save enough money for college. Danny isn't sure higher education is the right avenue for him, though. He seeks advice from Ty Webb (Chevy), a prominent member of the club. Ty essentially tells him to take drugs, then gives him the most Zen advice ever: "Be the ball."

Meanwhile, a loud, obnoxious club guest named Al Czervik (Dangerfield) shows up, treating the place as his own personal playground. He flirts with women, mocks the pretensions of the other members, and continually outrages the man who is perhaps the single greatest personification of the Bushwood spirit, Judge Elihu Smails (Ted Knight). Smails detests the outsider, who repeatedly tricks him into making bets he can't possibly win. Things between Czervik and Smails eventually come to a head. They seek advice from Ty, who suggests, naturally, a golf competition. Danny, having been briefly embraced by Smails, comes to see the man's hypocrisy, and the hypocrisy of Bushwood in general. Finally making sense of Ty's admonition to "be the ball," he sides with Czervik in the competition, ultimately making the winning shot. He has probably blown his chance at earning college money, but at least he knows what he stands for.

Occasionally rearing his head throughout the film is groundskeeper Carl Spackler (Murray), a slovenly sort who talks out of the corner of his mouth and watches lustfully as older female members bend over to pick up their balls. Carl is engaged in an increasingly futile fight against a persistent gopher that tears up the greens.

The characters played by Dangerfield, Murray, and Chevy were initially supposed to be of the supporting variety. Ramis, who also directed, knew they were giving him gold, though, so he ended up bringing them more front and center, according to an interview he did for the 20th anniversary DVD release.

Caddyshack gives Chevy one of his best roles. Ty Webb is an interesting contradiction: he is part of the Bushwood establishment, but not *of* it. As evidenced by his role as advice-giver, others (including Smails) view him as smart and knowledgeable, yet he does things like urinate on the course and subtly insult his colleagues. ("Don't sell yourself short, Judge. You're a tremendous slouch," he tells Smails.) Ty seems to live by the famous Groucho Marx line about not wanting to belong to any club that would have him as a member. The character plays on Chevy's inherent WASP-ness, allowing him to appear one way on the outside while embodying the exact opposite on the inside. One wonders if he might have known people like Ty Webb growing up, so perfectly does he nail the feeling of straddling the establishment line.

Ty is able to fit in because, in spite of a secret rebelliousness, he has his own set of prejudices. Whereas Smails shudders at Czervik's Jewishness and condescends to working class individuals at the club, Ty has more of a homophobic vibe. In one scene, he tells another character that he pretended to be "homo" in order to get out of serving in Vietnam. While the line comes off a bit flippant and offensive today, it does shed some light onto Ty. Perhaps, at some level, he knows that he has much in common with people like Smails. Perhaps his cavalier attitude toward Bushwood is an extension of some self-loathing he secretly carries.

When Ty is trying *not* to fit in, Chevy gets to engage in hijinks that are utterly hilarious and that show off the side of Ty that other Bushwooders would hate. These antics fit his style of comedy like a golf glove. During a sequence in which he beds Smails' niece, the suggestively named Lacey Underall (played by Cindy Morgan), he accidentally spills too much oil on her back and then slips off when he tries to mount her. It's a classic Chevy Chase bit, executed with crack precision. Same goes for the way he continually refers to Danny as "Timmy," and for the manner in which he croons a song of seduction to Lacey. The lyrics to his improvised opus: "I was born to love you. I was born to lick your face. I was born to rub you, but you were born to rub me first." Chevy's sly, off-the-cuff witticisms can also be found throughout *Caddyshack* ("Thank you very little." "Two wrongs don't make a right, but three rights make a left.")

Given that Chevy and Murray were huge stars, the filmmakers naturally wanted to find a way to give them a scene together. The two famously tussled backstage at *Saturday Night Live* when Chevy returned to host after his departure. Murray, egged on by pissed-off *SNL* cast members, confronted Chevy in a hallway. Words were exchanged, and the two nearly came to blows. Murray is said to have insulted Chevy by calling him "medium talent." Although they had presumably patched things up by the time *Caddyshack* went into production, there's still a noticeable comic tension between them; both know they're sharing the screen with a formidable funnyman, so they both up their game a little bit. The sequence is heavily ad-libbed – Ty chases a stray ball through Carl's stark abode – and presents two top comedians at play.

The combination of Chevy, Murray, and Dangerfield made *Caddyshack* a smash hit. While he gets less credit for its success, the film doubtlessly benefits from Ted Knight's brilliantly uptight performance; he earns at least as many laughs as any of his co-stars. (Chevy says in a DVD interview that he thinks Knight is the best thing in the movie.) The film may have veered slightly from its original story intentions, but it did so in all the right ways. For this reason, it is eminently re-watchable. No matter how many times its ardent fans – myself included – watch it, the laughs are still there. And in many respects, the "slobs vs. snobs" theme is just as relevant today as it was in 1980. As political and societal debates grow more and more contentious, both in person and online, the film's anti-establishment nature rings as meaningful as ever.

Despite having seen it numerous times over the years and counting it among my favorite comedies, I found that I had an interesting reaction after re-watching *Caddyshack* for the purposes of this book. For weeks afterward, I was absolutely obsessed with it, in a way I never had been before. I started quoting from it daily, and the Kenny Loggins theme song, "I'm Alright," became a much-repeated song on my car stereo. It occurred to me that *Caddyshack* is one of those movies that has had different meanings for me at different times in my life. In my earliest adolescent viewings, I loved the R-rated naughtiness, in addition to the anti-authority subject matter. By the time I was in my thirties, I noticed the construction of it more. Despite the broadness of the humor, it's a wonderfully acted film that contains some nicely-shot visual gags. Now, in my forties, I respond to the "screw the snobs" message. It reminds me of everyone who ever undeservedly took a superior position over me, and it makes me want to raise a metaphorical middle finger in salute to them. Rare are the comedies that can be looked at through different prisms. No wonder this one has achieved such intense fandom among so many.

Caddyshack II

Eight years after *Caddyshack*'s success, a follow-up was unleashed upon the public. Every so often, some website takes a poll to see what the worst sequel of all time is. Without fail, one that always seems to come in near or at the top is *Caddyshack II*. According to an interview Harold Ramis gave to The AV Club website, the film began as a tagline created by the studio: "The Shack is Back!" That the film did not warrant a sequel was beside the point; someone saw dollar signs and set the wheels in motion. This 1988 picture is a prime example of everything that's wrong with cinematic second parts. Even the people who made and star in it will tell you that it's terrible.

The studio wanted a sequel, but what do you do when most of the original players don't want to come back? In this case, they decided that **the formula itself** was the real star and set out to duplicate it as closely as possible. *Caddyshack II* takes a nebbishy good guy (Jonathan Silverman instead of Michael O'Keefe) and plunks him down in the middle of Bushwood Country Club. When Rodney Dangerfield – who was originally slated to star – backed out, they brought in another Borscht Belt comedian, Jackie Mason, to be the out-of-place "slob" who deflates the club's elitist "snobs." It subbed Robert Stack for the irreplaceable Ted Knight as the primary uptight snob. Since Murray didn't sign on, they brought in another *SNL* alum, Dan Aykroyd, to fulfill the "crazy" requirement. They even went so far as to have Kenny Loggins write and record a brand new theme song. While "Nobody's Fool" is perhaps not as iconic as the original's "I'm Alright," it certainly is one of the movie's few highlights.

Chevy was the only original cast member game enough for a sequel – or, more likely, an easy paycheck. He does the same "pretending to be one of the snobs while secretly mocking them" shtick from the first *Caddyshack,* although now the character has a decidedly weirder demeanor. We find Ty Webb heavily suntanned and with a stud in his ear. He gives the club members vulgar nicknames, such as "Mr. Crabs" and "Mr. Foreskin." (He never would have been so overtly disdainful in the original.) Ty also seems to have lost his finesse with the ladies. Whereas he once literally charmed the pants off Lacey Underall, he now strikes out with a table full of ladies after offending them with a variety of sexual euphemisms. It's almost like Ty Webb was kidnapped and replaced by an alien who was trying to pass as Ty Webb. The character simply isn't the same, and Chevy struggles to find something funny to do. If nothing else, he does get one classic bit in which he attempts to hang up a pool cue, only to knock a rack of them over.

Confession time: For a few years following its release, I actually kind of liked *Caddyshack II*. Not in a traditional way, mind you. This is a very bad picture, yet I was fascinated by its utter refusal to deviate from the formula. They theoretically could have gone a hundred different ways or told a brand new story about life at Bushwood, but they didn't. They doggedly held firm to the belief that by simply replicating as many elements from the original as closely as possible, they'd strike comic gold a second time. The movie even ends with a Ty Webb-recommended golf competition.

Director Allan Arkush and whoever re-wrote Ramis' screenplay not only did a Xerox copy, they also tried to amp up the tried-and-true factors they believed were key to the first one's success. The Jackie Mason character isn't just an obnoxious bore; he's an obnoxious bore who, in a fit of spite, buys Bushwood and turns it into a mini-golf course. And the gopher! He becomes a major character this time, now done with slightly more sophisticated (i.e. less funny) special effects. Seeing more of him dulls the impact.

My justification for initially liking *Caddyshack II* was that it's ultimately a movie about its own failed attempt at a franchise. It is an example of people desperately trying to catch lightning in a bottle twice. For me, that actually made some of the scenes humorous at the time. I didn't laugh because the comedy was of good quality (although Aykroyd's insistence on calling Stack "Mrs. Eszterhas" cracked me up); I laughed because the intention to duplicate the formula was so blatant that it became sublimely absurd. Comedy has always relied on the follies of clueless people. *Caddyshack II* doesn't have such follies in its plot, yet they permeate every single frame. In other words, any humor it contains comes not from the material but from the failed attempt at pulling the material off. I thought that, while it didn't work at the intended level, it did work on a whole other, unintended level.

Watching it again 20 years later, I no longer find it to be amusing on *any* level. Of course, I re-watched both *Caddyshack*s back-to-back, which certainly does the sequel no favors. Ramis' original had, at its core, a number of personal anecdotes about life as a teenage caddy that made it more relatable. The sequel is just forced. It completely loses the anarchic spirit of the first one. It has slobs and snobs, but not the underlying heart. The comedy is far too over-the-top, and the message about elitism is so overt that the comedy is suffocated.

Ty Webb's famous "be the ball" advice was all about following one's instincts to achieve success. *Caddyshack* knew how to be the ball, and ended up a comedic hole-in-one. *Caddyshack II* sliced into the woods.

Interesting trivia:

Caddyshack provided the loose inspiration for the 2007 hip-hop comedy *Who's Your Caddy*, which detailed the attempts of a rap mogul to join a snooty country club. The film, which starred Outkast's Big Boi, was a critical and financial flop.

Caddyshack II features a young actress named Chynna Phillips, who would go on to find more fame as a singer, as part of the '90s pop group Wilson Phillips.

As of this writing, *Caddyshack II* has exactly one fresh rating on Rotten Tomatoes. That review was written by yours truly. While I don't believe the movie is good, I did pen a deconstructionist critique of the movie (making the same points I made above) as an exercise in stirring up discussion about a movie that's widely recognized as terrible. If nothing else, it lifted the movie's Tomatometer score from 0% to 8%.

Seems Like Old Times

After the success of *Foul Play*, it's little surprise that a studio wanted to re-team Chevy and Goldie Hawn, or that the two stars wanted to work together again. Their second and final collaboration was 1980's *Seems Like Old Times*, a romantic farce penned by Neil Simon.

The movie has a truly bizarre premise when you think about it. Chevy plays Nick Gardenia, a down-on-his-luck writer who, as the story opens, is working on his latest project in a mountain cabin. A couple of guys knock on the door and force Nick to get in their car. They take him to a bank, give him an unloaded gun, and make him perform a stick-up. In the process, he ends up looking right into the security camera. Nick escapes the criminals' clutches and, knowing the cops will be looking for him, seeks out the one person he knows he can turn to for help: his ex-wife Glenda Parks (Hawn). In an act of pure cinematic contrivance, Glenda is a public defender who hires all her clients as household help to keep them out of further trouble. She's also married to the Los Angeles District Attorney, Ira Parks (Charles Grodin).

Once this setup is in place, *Seems Like Old Times* proceeds to deliver a series of shamelessly forced bits of humor, as Glenda desperately tries to keep Ira from discovering that she's hiding Nick in the room above the garage. Ira, you see, is actively trying to locate the reluctant bank robber. There's also the little matter of Glenda experiencing some rekindled feelings for Nick, and vice versa. The entire third act of the picture has Ira learning the truth, but unable to do anything about it because he's hosting a dinner party for the Governor. When one of Glenda's clients, who was supposed to be working as a waiter, passes out drunk, Nick dons a jacket and ends up serving food to two of the very men who are trying to put him behind bars.

The ending of the movie ranks among the worst ever committed to a major film. During Nick's trial, a pack of dogs is accidentally unleashed in the courtroom while the exasperated judge looks on. Nick proves himself innocent and immediately tries to make a play for Glenda, who rejects him. In the final scene, Glenda and Ira head out on a trip in an attempt to repair their now-shaky marriage. Driving in the rain, they swerve to avoid hitting a cow that has materialized in the middle of the road, and end up crashing. Because Ira is injured, Glenda goes for help. She comes upon a cabin and knocks on the door, only to have Nick answer. It's the same cabin he was in at the beginning of the movie. Glenda smiles, at which point the image freeze-frames and the credits roll. Think about this for a second. Are we to believe that Glenda will make the decision to leave her husband for another man while he lies injured in a wrecked car? Kind of cold, don't you think?

Seems Like Old Times was a moderate success in 1980 and, as of this writing, it still maintains a 75% approval rating on Rotten Tomatoes. I remember watching it often as a kid, getting much amusement from the wacky twists and turns of the plot. Seen again today, the movie strikes me as severely dated. The tone definitely feels like something out of the late '70s/early '80s, with jokes pitched at the level of an era-appropriate sitcom. Many of the scenarios are handled that way too. (Dogs in a courtroom for a laugh? Really?) It doesn't help that director Jay Sandrich stages everything in a flat, stagey manner that belies his extensive sitcom work on shows like *The Mary Tyler Moore Show* and *Benson*. What works visually on TV doesn't necessarily cut it on the big screen. Sandrich's direction undermines a lot of the jokes, making them feel like scripted gags rather than actual human conversation or interaction.

Neil Simon has written a lot of great things in his time, but, like David Mamet, not everyone can successfully translate his words. That's certainly true of *Seems Like Old Times*. Consequently, it feels like everyone is making a different movie. Sandrich is unable to guide his cast to a unified comedic style. Charles Grodin – who probably comes off best – is wisely playing everything straight, as though not in a comedy, which makes his scenes funniest. Hawn approaches her role as though the picture is a retro screwball romance.

Chevy, meanwhile, doesn't really play a character so much as he just does his own bits. There are pratfalls and physical gags aplenty here, along with several dozen of his patented bits of verbal sarcasm. It isn't that he's not funny, it's more that he tries to adapt his own brand of comedy to Neil Simon's script. While both men are capable of creating uproarious material, Chevy and Simon are not necessarily a logical match. The writer is known for an often humane style of humor, whereas Chevy, at this point in his career at least, focused primarily on exaggerated silliness.

Regardless of the goodness of fit, there is one indisputably great moment in the film. Nick hides under a bed when Ira comes into the room. Unbeknownst to Ira, he is stepping on Nick's finger, which protrudes ever so slightly. The scene shows only Chevy's hands, as he tries to use the one not pinned down by Ira's foot to signal Glenda. Few people can be funny using only their hands, and Chevy is one of them.

What I found revisiting *Seems Like Old Times* is that it has inspired individual moments that don't add up to a satisfying whole. I remembered the movie with great fondness, only to find that it doesn't hold up especially well. Individual jokes intermittently strike a chord, but the clunky wheels of the plot grind down the light-on-its-feet rhythm a romantic-comedy like this needs.

In terms of the larger picture of Chevy's career, this is not a great role, nor is it a terrible one. Collaborating again with Goldie Hawn certainly earned both of them some goodwill from the public and, whether seamlessly integrated into the story or not, there are ample opportunities for him to indulge in his strengths. Nonetheless, *Seems Like Old Times* is not a movie that typically jumps directly to mind when Chevy's name is invoked. It was a decent-enough comedy in 1980; today, it just feels more like a relic from another era rather than something that endures.

Under the Rainbow

When it was released in 1981, *Under the Rainbow* was a critical and commercial bomb. It garnered some of the worst reviews of the year, while also racking up a couple of Razzie awards. The movie quickly became a staple of cable TV – and a convenient punchline. I watched it frequently on HBO as an adolescent. While no one (even a 13 year-old) would mistake it for a good movie, I recall thinking that the premise was actually pretty ambitious, even if the execution wasn't entirely successful.

Set in 1938, the movie follows the exploits of several different characters, all of whom converge upon a Hollywood hotel. Chevy plays U.S. Secret Service agent Bruce Thorpe, who is attempting to protect an Austrian royal duke (Joseph Maher) and duchess (Eve Arden) from an assassin. Billy Barty portrays Otto Kriegling, a Nazi agent who has come to Hollywood to pass along American military secrets to a Japanese spy. Then there's Carrie Fisher as Annie Clark, a movie studio "gopher" assigned to corral the hundreds of little people hired to work on a new picture called *The Wizard of Oz*. One of the people she's charged with minding is Rollo Sweet (Cork Hubbert), a little person with dreams of big-time stardom. As Kriegling and the assassin attempt to carry out their respective goals, the other characters all bounce off one another in various combinations.

Under the Rainbow is a farce, and farces are notoriously difficult to pull off on-screen. Timing is everything. The movie gets the mayhem right, but never quite nails that timing. For a farce to be successful, it needs to have an almost effortless flow. The audience should be so swept up in the pace that they never notice the wheels turning. *Under the Rainbow* makes you notice the wheels almost constantly. So many of the plot complications feel forced. An excess of characters – including the hotel's hapless assistant manager (Adam Arkin) – compounds the problem, never giving the viewer time to cozy up to any of them.

Only in the last half hour do things improve. Suddenly, the film starts to tie everything together, capping off with a wild chase through a studio backlot. Sure, that kind of thing has been done before, but it's always kind of fun, right?

As a vehicle for Chevy Chase, *Under the Rainbow* remains as much a curiosity as *Oh! Heavenly Dog*. Despite being prodigiously funny, he essentially plays straight-man to everyone else. Bruce Thorpe is easily the least wacky character in the whole picture. There are moments in which Chevy tries to insert a little bit of his trademark humor, yet director Steve Rash never allows him room to cut loose. The role could have been played by at least a dozen other stars of the time; why anyone thought of Chevy for it – or why he thought of *himself* for it – remains a mystery.

There were five credited screenwriters on the project, indicating that the script was heavily rewritten. One of them, Martin Smith, was primarily a documentarian who specialized in WWII-era history. (Presumably, he contributed to the Kriegling subplot.) Another writer was Pat McCormick, the comedian who wrote material for Jack Paar, appeared regularly on *The Gong Show*, and was a staple of the Friars Club roasts. McCormick was the epitome of the show-biz generation Chevy and crew rebelled against so mercilessly with *Saturday Night Live*. To see him trapped in the middle of outdated schtick is a bizarre sight, indeed. There's a moment in which we see a bus filled with camera-toting Japanese tourists. The sign on the bus reads "Japanese Amateur Photography Society," i.e. JAPS. Another quasi-racist gag centers around a secret code phrase Kriegling is supposed to hear from his contact: "The pearl is in the river." Instead, he encounters one of the Japanese shutterbugs who, noticing the Duchess has dropped a jewel in her dinner, exclaims,

"The pearl is in the liver!" While one cannot say for certain that McCormick wrote these bits, it's probably safe to assume that Martin Smith did not.

In its day, *Under the Rainbow* was expected to be a comedy hit; when people saw that it didn't work, they wrote it off as a complete failure. While it may, in fact, be a failure, it's an ambitious failure – one that has its fair share of pleasures. Some of the throwaway lines are rather funny, as are several of the sight gags, such as a recurring bit in which the Duke keeps accidentally killing his wife's dog, then replacing it with one that looks nothing like the previous one. There's also something clever about the way the movie pays tribute to *The Wizard of Oz* by co-opting its structure (the events shown turn out to be Rollo's dream after sustaining an injury; the other characters are actually his friends and loved ones).

Over the years, *Under the Rainbow* has amassed something of a cult following. The many disparate elements it contains are undoubtedly a big reason why. Love it or hate it, there is nothing else quite like it. Rarely have so many mismatched people and components been assembled in such a curious way.

Interesting Trivia: Chevy met his third wife, the former Jayni Luke, on the set of *Under the Rainbow*. She worked on the film as a production coordinator. They've been together ever since.

Modern Problems

If there's one movie in his filmography that Chevy probably wishes he'd never made, it's 1981's *Modern Problems*. His likely reason for wishing he could unmake the picture has nothing to do with its lack of quality and everything to do with a near-fatal accident on the set. For a dream sequence in which his character, air traffic controller Max Fielding, envisions himself as an airplane, Chevy had a string of landing lights attached to his body. The padding used to protect him wasn't strong enough, and when the power was flipped on, electric current ran through the muscles in his arms, neck, and back, nearly killing him. Afterward, he fell into a deep depression. Chevy told biographer Rena Fruchter (in her book *I'm Chevy Chase...and You're Not*) that he couldn't turn a light switch on or off for a year, so traumatized was he.

This incident is almost as bad as what happens to the character he plays. Max Fielding is in his car, unlucky enough to be behind a tanker truck that is spilling toxic waste all over the road. After being doused with the stuff, he discovers that he not only glows in the dark but also has the ability to make things happen with the power of his mind. Some people would take this as a miracle. Not Max. He's already sullen and depressed, thanks to being dumped by girlfriend Darcy (Patti D'Arbanville). His job is none too satisfying either. Max sees his newfound abilities as a liability rather than an asset.

Things come to a head when he and Darcy are invited to the beach house owned by an acquaintance, author Mark Winslow (Dabney Coleman). Obnoxious and intimidating, Winslow thinks nothing of putting Max down or making him feel even more self-conscious. During a fancy dinner, Max finally snaps. He becomes so enraged that he loses whatever control of his powers he may have had. Suddenly, he begins violently flinging Winslow around the dining room before placing him face-first in a bowl of mashed potatoes. Despondent at the monster he's become, Max decides to end it all by climbing to the top of Winslow's house during a severe thunderstorm. Darcy, finally realizing how much she loves the guy, climbs up too, hoping to talk him down. In the movie's final moments, Max is struck by lightning, which somehow transfers his powers to Winslow's voodoo-obsessed maid (Nell Carter).

Modern Problems reunited Chevy with director/co-writer Ken Shapiro, with whom he made *The Groove Tube*. Their second, and last, collaboration yielded very odd results. I've seen this film a number of times over the years, and despite some inspired moments, it never really gets any better or more coherent.

Shapiro's first mistake was trying to be timely without having any perspective. It was probably coincidence that the 1981 air traffic controller's strike occurred just five months before the film's release, but the idea of Max getting covered in toxic waste was clearly inspired by nuclear fears generated by the Three Mile Island incident of two years prior. (Unrelated Note: I live a very short distance from Three Mile Island, and have even visited there. Our lovely area appears to be safe.) Exploiting the nuclear paranoia seems like brilliant fodder for a satire, yet *Modern Problems* says nothing about it. Shapiro uses the concept simply as a quick way to explain Max's sudden powers. There is no greater comic notion at play, which immediately robs the movie of what could have been its greatest strength.

Things start off promisingly. While the film's theme song, "Gonna Get It Next Time" by The Tubes, plays on the soundtrack, Max drives home from work, a variety of humorous, everyday annoyances ruining his trip: his sunroof won't close, the tape deck eats his cassette, he scratches his car trying to park it. The scene where he realizes Darcy is serious about leaving him is funny, too; Max shakes her diaphragm box and is horrified to find it empty. A vintage bit of Chevy comedy also comes as Max first discovers his abilities. He loses his grip on the soap while showering, sending it flying into the cat litter box. He magically lifts it out of the box, turns on the sink, and washes it off.

Then things start to take a darker turn. Despite being told he is "a prince who thinks he's a frog," Max begins exhibiting traits of negativity and jealousy. He semi-stalks Darcy, often groveling for her to come back. These scenes aren't funny. Max is kind of creepy, without being lovable. His low self-esteem fuels his magic powers even further, which in turn sends him over the edge. *Modern Problems* is a comedy about a man going down the drain, albeit one that doesn't attempt to make his descent all that empathetic. And, oddly, the stranger he acts, the more Darcy wants him, which doesn't make sense. Then again, she may be deluded by the multiple "magic" orgasms he gives her after they end up in bed together. This particular bit is a fine example of what the movie needed more of. It shows Max using his gifts to create a bogus sense of his own competence. Most of the time, he's just insufferably mopey.

Modern Problems never figures out exactly what it wants to be. Individual scenes are clever, but the film as a whole never generates a pulse. The pace goes flat when it should be quickening. Shapiro obviously has some inventive ideas. He just doesn't know how to incorporate them all together. Max's unhappiness pervades too much of the story when, in reality, it should merely be complimenting the gags.

The reach of the director's ideas also exceed his grasp. This is most notable in the climactic dinner party scene. While Max is hurling Winslow around the room – a sight that would leave any normal human aghast – the other characters stand motionless, watching things unfold as though witnessing a televised golf match. Shapiro undersells the value of reaction, one of the most powerful tools in the comedy toolkit. Because of this, the alleged comic highlight of the movie doesn't pay off.

For his part, Chevy seems disengaged much of the time. It is hard to tell if that's just his interpretation of the character, if he was unhappy with the material, or if it was a result of the accident. Only in little bursts does he come alive. The best-known moment of *Modern Problem*s is a great example of his occasional flickering. The maid attempts to exorcise the now demonically-crazed Max by spreading some kind of voodoo powder around his bed. Taking it as a challenge, Max gets on the floor and snorts it all up, cocaine-style, before maniacally exclaiming, "I like it!"

Modern Problems opened at Christmastime, doing $26 million at the box office. While Chevy's star power carried it a little way, toxic word of mouth could not be contained. The movie has cult appeal for some viewers to this day, although in the larger scheme of Chevy's career, it is considered to be one of his more notorious flops. He's not really to blame, though. Ken Shapiro was, by and large, an untested director (he never helmed another film), working from a screenplay that was, at best, unfocused. Shapiro also didn't really know how to use Chevy's considerable talents. Of course, the electrocution could have played a part as well. One cannot say how much it affected Chevy's morale, or the rest of the crew's. The movie was probably intended to be edgy and topical; for whatever reason, it ended up disjointed and strangely unsettling.

The Vacation Movies

National Lampoon's Vacation

There is one character that Chevy Chase is most closely identified with: Clark W. Griswold. *National Lampoon's Vacation*, released in 1983, first introduced America to Griswold and his family. John Hughes wrote the initial screenplay, based on his National Lampoon article "Vacation '58," which detailed a disastrous family car trip from the perspective of one of the kids in the back seat. Director Harold Ramis rewrote the script (and a version exists that also lists Chevy as a co-writer) to shift the POV from that of the kids to that of the hapless father. The shift worked magically. *Vacation* draws inspiration from something everyone can relate to: the family getaway that ends up being anything but relaxing. Finding humor in such a relatable subject made the movie an instant hit and, over time, a legitimate comedy classic.

The premise is simple: Clark Griswold wants to take his wife Ellen (Beverly D'Angelo), son Rusty (Anthony Michael Hall), and daughter Audrey (Dana Barron) on a trip to Walley World, America's most beloved amusement park (and a thinly-veiled Disneyland stand-in). Despite his family's protestations, Clark refuses to fly there. Instead, he buys a station wagon that he dubs "the Griswold family truckster" and insists they drive cross-country. Numerous mishaps occur, including the death of Aunt Edna (Imogene Coca), who accompanies them for part of the trip. There's also an unfortunate visit to the home of "Cousin Eddie" (Randy Quaid), the dictionary definition of white trash. Clark also finds himself engaging in a flirtation with a fellow traveler, played by model Christie Brinkley. After finally getting to Walley World, the Griswolds discover that it is temporarily closed for repairs. Clark, exasperated by the Murphy's Law nature of his family's journey, can no longer take it. He gets a gun and forces a security guard (John Candy) to open the park for them. The park's owner and namesake, Roy Walley (Eddie Bracken), is called to the scene. A family man himself, he empathizes with Clark's plight and agrees not to press charges. The movie ends with the Griswolds, Walley, and the park security team enjoying a roller coaster ride.

The masterstroke of *National Lampoon's Vacation* is that it spoofs the all-American, Norman Rockwell-esque vision of life. Clark Griswold yearns for that kind of perfection and simplicity, only to find it repeatedly out of his reach. The movie's humor is built upon a mounting sense of desperation; Clark is adamant about giving his family an old-fashioned good time, but the harder he tries, the more things spiral out of control. *Vacation* is a film about idealism vs. reality, about the way what we envision in our minds is often wildly different from how things really play out. Much like *Caddyshack* – which had a relevant theme of elitism running beneath the hijinks – *Vacation* works not just because of the wacky humor, but because of the identifiable ideas that inform that humor.

By the time *Vacation* was released in 1983, the United States was a different place. The country had gone through notable changes courtesy of the Vietnam War, the Watergate scandal, and the sexual revolution. Old-fashioned ideas of what America looked like had gone out the window, replaced by a combination of cynicism and liberation. Entertainment had grown edgier, with clean-cut '70s performers like John Denver and The

Carpenters replaced by the makeup-wearing KISS and a barrage of funky-looking New Wave groups from Great Britain. TV was still often cheesy, yet there was a new-found frankness in subject matter, with shows milking humor from hitherto untouched topics such as promiscuity and homosexuality. Movies were edgier too, tacking subjects like workplace inequality (*9 to 5*), adolescent sexuality (*Porky's* and *The Blue Lagoon*), and the very scandals that rocked the country a few years earlier (*The China Syndrome, All the President's Men*). Despite President Ronald Reagan pushing a form of values left over from the 1950s, there was a sense that – to paraphrase Bob Dylan – things had changed.

While it is in no way a political film, *Vacation* certainly benefited from being released in that time period. Clark Griswold represents the idea that the "simplicity"of an earlier era is ideal, and everything that happens to his family en route to Walley World represents the fact that cultural regression simply isn't possible. There is no such thing as a quaint family car trip anymore – not when the destinations are all commercial enterprises, the guy selling you a new car is out to screw you, and you can't even stop to ask for directions without getting your car jacked. *Get with the times*, the movie seems to say, *and accept that you're never going to be Pat Boone or Ward Cleaver.*

Chevy really understood the comic center of the film, creating a character who is charmingly naive in his optimism. Only when he breaks down and accepts the hopelessness of his situation do things start to go his way. He literally has to snap before he can accept that "imperfections" don't necessarily rob his family's trip of meaning. If anything, they're bonded more closely because of all they've endured. Part of the reason Clark Griswold has permanently entered the pop culture lexicon is that Chevy made him palpably real. Clark is a good man with admirable goals. He deserves to succeed and doesn't grasp that he's his own worst enemy.

There are many other notable treats to be found in *Vacation*. One of the greatest is the chemistry between Chevy and Beverly D'Angelo. As I've stated previously, he didn't always have chemistry with female co-stars. D'Angelo, even more than Goldie Hawn, was a perfect match for him. Her Ellen Griswold is equal parts adoring and frustrated. While she might grow exasperated with Clark's antics, she also sees the decency behind them, which prevents her from ever getting *too* mad at him - even when he has a rendezvous with Christie Brinkley in a motel swimming pool.

The performance of Randy Quaid as Cousin Eddie is another highlight. Just as the Griswolds take a detour to visit Eddie and his clan's home, so does the film take a detour. Quaid creates an indelible character, a guy who is slovenly and repellant, yet also oddly endearing. The scenes set at his abode showcase some of the screenplay's most outrageous jokes. Eddie's daughter Vicki confesses to Audrey that she knows how to French kiss. When Audrey suggests that most teenage girls know how to do this, Vicki replies, "Yeah, but Daddy says I'm the best at it." The depiction of "white trash" life, meanwhile, is fairly pointed. Eddie serves Hamburger Helper without the hamburger ("It's just fine by itself!") and apparently grills his buns, while his daughter stirs a pitcher of Kool-Aid by sticking her whole arm in it and swirling it around.

National Lampoon's Vacation holds up marvelously. There are wall-to-wall laughs, with Ramis maintaining just the right tone throughout. While much has changed since the early '80s, there are still people who yearn for a more innocent, Rockwell-esque way of life. In fact, given that children today often seem disconnected from their families due to the cell phones and other electronic devices they are often absorbed with, it's possible that the movie is more relevant than ever.

National Lampoon's European Vacation

Given the success of *Vacation*, it's no wonder that a sequel was quickly put into production and released two years later. *European Vacation* had some critical changes in the production team, which, from a quality standpoint, turned out to be detrimental. Harold Ramis did not return to direct, nor did he contribute to the screenplay. Amy Heckerling (*Fast Times at*

Ridgemont High) took over helming duties instead. The writing is credited to John Hughes and Robert Klane; little of Hughes' personal touch can be found in the script, but Klane's brand of bombastic dopiness (he scripted *Weekend at Bernie's* and the Tom Selleck fiasco *Folks!*) is pervasive. And because Anthony Michael Hall had become a star since the first *Vacation* was released, he opted to take the lead role in *Weird Science* instead of reprising the role of Rusty. As such, new actors were cast as the Griswold children. This would soon become a joke in the series, but we'll get to that a little later.

It's apparent in the opening moments that *European Vacation* will abandon the relatable feel of the original. It starts with the Griswolds in a very *un*-relatable situation. They are appearing on a TV game show called "Pig in a Poke." Ridiculously dressed in pig costumes, they are peppered with unfair questions that seem to give an edge to their opponents. But then the Griswold family fails upward, as Ellen accidentally gives the right answer to the final question. The grand prize they receive is, of course, an all-expenses paid trip to Europe. Already, the *Vacation* premise has gone out the window. Instead of Clark trying to plan something wonderful for his family, the sequel painfully contrives a way to get them on a trip. Even worse, it stops for *four* dream sequences, as each Griswold imagines what the vacation might be like. For Clark, it's something akin to *The Sound of Music.*

Once in Europe, the movie does little more than march them through one country after another, inadvertently wreaking havoc wherever they go. Some of the situations the Griswolds find themselves in are flat-out stupid. For instance, Clark takes a video of Ellen in the shower. His camcorder is later stolen, and the footage is used to advertise an Italian porn flick. Even worse is a subplot involving a thief; the third act of *European Vacation* finds the clan in the midst of a caper, and the grand finale has Ellen being kidnapped. This leads to a chase that pays off with Clark driving a car into one of Rome's famed fountains. Interestingly, this is the second comedy, after *Oh! Heavenly Dog,* in which Chevy goes to Europe and gets involved in some sort of caper. Thankfully, he at least remains in human form this time.

Whereas the original *Vacation* was a comically exaggerated version of a very identifiable idea – father wants to create a memorable experience with his family – *European Vacation* is nothing but shtick. The humor is poorly conceived in parts, most notably in regard to a recurring character played by Eric Idle. Apparently, someone thought it would be a good idea to get a Monty Python alum in the picture, so Idle shows up periodically (and often inexplicably) so that Clark Griswold can run him over with a car or trap him in the revolving door of a hotel. Seeing Chase and Idle together on screen should promise huge laughs, yet the material they are given is cheap, predictable, and not especially witty.

Another significant problem is that the Griswold kids have had complete personality changes. Audrey (now played by Dana Hill) is a neurotic mess, constantly worried about whether her studly boyfriend back home is cheating on her. She's also portrayed as having an eating disorder. Although very slender in the original, the character here is heavier, and the movie tries to find comedy in a cruel dream sequence in which Audrey eats everything in sight until she puffs up like a blimp. Rusty (Jason Lively), meanwhile, has gone from an adolescent boy trying to identify with his dad to a stereotypical horndog, sneaking out to pick up foreign women in a club. By changing the personalities of the Griswold children, *European Vacation* alters a crucial dynamic that helped make its predecessor popular.

Since the family is traveling through Europe, there are a lot of landmarks referenced, to varying degrees of success. One of the film's only laugh-out-loud bits finds Clark unable to merge in traffic and getting stuck in a roundabout. ("Look, kids! Big Ben! Parliament!" he says repeatedly, offering one of the few memorable lines of dialogue.) In a later scene, the family arrives at the Louvre fifteen minutes before it closes. Not wanting to admit defeat, Clark insists they rush though it, looking at each piece of artwork for only about half a second. Less successful is a bit in which he backs a car into Stonehenge, causing the landmark to topple like a set of dominoes. I've never been to Europe, but I have a sneaking suspicion that you aren't allowed to get a car that close to Stonehenge. A sequence set atop the Eiffel

Tower is similarly bereft of ideas, going to great lengths to – hold onto your hats here, folks – have a woman's dog jump off.

Some sequences are visibly contrived, yet still give Chevy a chance to shine. While traipsing through Germany, the clan stumbles upon an Oktoberfest celebration. Clark, fully in the spirit, puts on a pair of lederhosen and gets onstage to participate in a dance. Chevy executes the early part of the scene brilliantly, as Clark struggles to keep up with the other male dancers, all of whom actually know the correct movements. Perpetually wearing an idiotic grin designed to emphasize Clark's satisfaction with his own perceived worldliness, Chevy makes the scene a masterfully executed piece of physical comedy, especially after the dance evolves into a fistfight thanks to Clark's clumsy movements.

European Vacation has its fans, and there are certainly some worthy moments scattered throughout. In terms of Chevy's career, it falls somewhere in the middle. It is neither his best nor his worst film. That said, it marks a substantial drop-off from the original. The *Vacation* series is at its best when Clark Griswold is desperate for perfection. He's not doing that this time. There are a few casual mentions of his desire to make it a great trip, but Amy Heckerling, although talented, doesn't really understand the necessary rhythm. There are jokes aplenty, but none of the heart that rested beneath Ramis' picture. Whereas *Vacation* builds to its satisfying conclusion, this sequel fizzles out. The last scene finds the family returning to the United States. When bumbling Clark distracts the pilots, the airplane smashes into the Statue of Liberty's torch, knocking it askew. The original ended with a freeze frame of everyone on a roller coaster. One ending is spot-on, the other a cheap bit of comedy that stands for nothing.

National Lampoon's Christmas Vacation

December 1, 1989 brought the release of the third installment in the series, *National Lampoon's Christmas Vacation*. Initially, the movie was met with mockery because this was the one where *the Griswolds don't actually take a vacation!*

There was a fairly widespread assumption that it was a lazy cash grab, only a notch above the umpteenth *Police Academy* sequel. But whereas *European Vacation* showed it would betray the spirit of the franchise in its first scene, *Christmas Vacation* proudly made it clear that it would bring that spirit back, even if the family *was* just staying home. We catch up with the Griswolds as they drive into the woods to cut down the "perfect" Christmas tree. Ellen, Audrey, and Rusty just want to get one at a store, but the idealistic Clark insists on giving his brood an old-fashioned holiday experience. He ends up pulling a massive tree from the ground. The tree is so large that it weighs down the car when he straps it to the roof. From this introduction, *Christmas Vacation* proceeds to recapture the magic of the original while still finding its own niche. The fact that they go nowhere doesn't matter, because the movie is hysterically funny.

The plot begins with Clark waiting for a Christmas bonus, which he will use to put in a swimming pool. Meanwhile, his parents and in-laws all descend on the Griswold home for a holiday celebration. This brings a number of stresses: a squirrel hiding in the tree gets loose inside the house, the turkey served for dinner is too dry, and the lights strung over every square inch of the house won't light up. Then Cousin Eddie and his clan show up unannounced. Eddie tells Clark that they're living in the RV they arrived in. One morning, Clark awakens to find Eddie emptying the RV's septic system into a public sewer. "Merry Christmas!" Eddie yells. "The shitter's full!" (This is perhaps the most quotable line of dialogue in any of the *Vacation* pictures.) When the boss stiffs Clark on the bonus, instead enrolling him in the "Jelly of the Month" club, he flips his lid. Eddie, wanting to be helpful, kidnaps the boss and delivers him to the Griswold living room. (Shades of the family forcing their way into Walley World, no?) Clark confronts his boss and, in the end, everything is resolved. He gets his bonus, plus an additional twenty percent.

Christmas Vacation, like its predecessor, had some notable changes both behind and in front of the camera. The screenplay is credited only to John Hughes and does not appear to have been rewritten by anyone else. (It's very likely that Chevy did some improvisation, though.) The director is Jeremiah

Chechik, an award-winning commercial director who made his feature film debut here. (Chechik went on to direct the Johnny Depp film *Benny & Joon* and a couple other minor pictures. His big screen career ended after his Sean Connery-starring *The Avengers* became one of the most notorious flops in Hollywood history. He now is a prolific TV director.) As was par for the course, two new actors were hired to play the Griswold children. A pre-*Cape Fear* Juliette Lewis plays Audrey, who has been reinstated to her more innocent – and skinny – self. Rusty is played by Johnny Galecki, who would later find fame on the TV shows *Roseanne* and *The Big Bang Theory*. Once again, Rusty is a boy who looks up to his dad. He also seems to be a little younger than he was in *European Vacation*.

The yuletide season is a perfect match for this series. The original established Clark's craving for picture-postcard perfection, and what could be more idealized than Christmas? We've all seen the images he wants to make reality – snow on the ground, fire in the fireplace, colored lights in the trees. Such images have been burned into our collective consciousness by artists such as Norman Rockwell and Thomas Kinkade, not to mention sundry Hallmark card designers. These things appeal to Clark, and his repeatedly foiled attempts to make them real for Ellen and the kids gives the movie the exact same comic punch that going to Walley World did.

One of the highlights is a running joke about the Christmas lights Clark strings across the house. He spends a large chunk of the film trying to get them to work (and occasionally falling off the roof in the process). Anyone who has ever strung lights will know that feeling. Clark becomes increasingly infuriated. The punchline is that when he does eventually get them going, he lights up the entire neighborhood, blinds his neighbors, sends the electricity meter on his house spinning wildly, and eventually taps out the power grid. The way the humor centers around his quest for "perfection" - and the complicated results that quest brings - makes *Christmas Vacation* a worthy successor to the premise established by the original.

The story's look at family relations is equally capable of spurring identification. Who *hasn't* been annoyed by their family at Christmas? Spending the holiday with one's relatives sounds wonderful. The reality can sometimes be different. Clark and Ellen's parents are opinionated, meddling, and cranky. Cousin Eddie is predictably gauche, going so far as to wear a fake red turtleneck underneath a white t-shirt, not to mention to whole thing about the shitter being full. It's interesting to note that extended family members are critical to the success of this franchise. The two best installments – the original and this one – both include Griswold relatives as supporting characters. *European Vacation* and *Vegas Vacation* (which we'll get to in a minute) are widely considered the lesser installments. The former had no relatives at all, while the latter did include Cousin Eddie, but more out of obligation than inspiration.

Christmas Vacation allows Chevy to deliver one of his warmest performances. There are multiple opportunities for him to engage in his trademark physical comedy. For example, a bit in which Clark is sticky with tree sap and therefore unable to turn the pages of a magazine without ripping them is gold. At the same time, the screenplay also allows for Clark to show a range of emotions. He is, by turns, excited to spend a magical holiday with his beloved family, annoyed by his inability to get the seasonal trappings right, befuddled by Cousin Eddie and the in-laws, outraged at his boss' cheapness, and, finally, resigned to have a joyous Christmas in spite of a few imperfections. Chevy skillfully plays all these emotions in a comic manner, once again using them in the creation of a character who is lovable for his sincerity and optimism.

Vacation ends with Clark getting what he wants: a trip to Walley World. *European Vacation* doesn't give him any satisfaction; the film ends with everyone gladly returning to the United States after a disastrous sojourn abroad. *Christmas Vacation* corrects this problem by again giving the character some joy – once he's learned to stop obsessing over perfection, that is. The last shot of the picture is Clark standing in front of his brightly lit house, smiling. "I did it," he says with pride. Through all the strife, he still managed to create a memorable Christmas for Ellen and the kids. A major key to the effectiveness of a *Vacation* movie is that Clark is foiled for 99% of the time, then allowed to feel a sliver of pleasure. Having him tormented for 90 minutes, as *European Vacation* did, robbed that film of any emotional satisfaction. While a healthy dose of cynicism is essential for the sake of comedy, we like Clark and want to see him have "the hap-hap-happiest Christmas since Bing Crosby tap danced with Danny-fucking-Kaye." In the four-film franchise, he's probably never happier than he is at the end here. No wonder it's gone on to become a modern holiday classic.

Vegas Vacation

Although *Christmas Vacation* was the highest-grossing entry in the series, it took eight years before the Griswolds would hit the big screen again. As per custom, more changes were happening behind the camera. *Vegas Vacation*, released February 14, 1997, is the only chapter that doesn't bear the National Lampoon name in its title. It's the only one without John Hughes' involvement as well. By this point in his career, Hughes had rather famously begun his retreat into retirement. He hadn't directed a picture since 1991's *Curly Sue*, and the few produced screenplays he wrote (remakes of *Miracle on 34th Street, Flubber,* and *101 Dalmatians*) showed heavy signs of boredom on his part, as they lacked the comic snap and human soul that exemplified his best work. The screenplay (eventually rewritten) is credited to a television writer named Elisa Bell, with a story credit going to her and Bob Ducsay. It is an unusual collaboration, considering that Ducsay is not a writer, but a film editor who cut such pictures as the low-budget Renee Zellweger crime thriller *Love and a .45* and Disney's live-action remake of *The Jungle Book.* Sitting in the director's chair for *Vegas Vacation* was Stephen Kessler, making his feature debut.

Yet another alteration in the series came with casting. Rusty and Audrey are now teenagers and once again played by new actors (Ethan Embry and Marisol Nichols). At least this particular recurring change is mocked in the film itself, when

Clark looks at his children and says, "You guys are growing up so fast, I hardly recognize you anymore."

Vegas Vacation opens with Clark driving home from work having just received a big raise. He sings along to the Beach Boys' "Good Vibrations" in the car. (It's a silly moment that lets Chevy go comically nuts with the song.) Once home, Clark announces that he's taking everyone to Vegas. They board a plane and make their way to Sin City. It is, to say the least, an eventful excursion. Clark becomes a gambling addict, losing a ton of money in the process. Rusty, meanwhile, hits jackpot after jackpot, eventually winning four brand new cars. Ellen is wooed by Wayne Newton, while Audrey turns into a Vegas party girl. Just when it seems things couldn't be worse, Cousin Eddie shows up. He tries to help Clark win back his money, to no avail. The movie ends with Ellen ditching Newton, and the family driving home in the cars Rusty won.

There are some very funny moments in *Vegas Vacation.* In arguably the best of them, Clark convinces Ellen to join the "Mile High Club" on the plane to Vegas. The airplane restroom turns out to be too small. As the couple tries to fool around, Ellen gets her leg stuck in the toilet. Clark reaches in to free her. The film then cuts to them getting out of a cab in front of the hotel. Ellen's pant leg and Clark's arm are covered in the blue toilet liquid. Another good bit finds Audrey hanging out a limousine's sunroof while tooling down the Strip. Clark accidentally closes the sunroof, pinning his daughter. After finally being released, Audrey lifts up her shirt to reveal a huge red mark across her stomach.

Moments like these are very much in the *Vacation* spirit. Others are not quite as successful. A senseless cameo from Christie Brinkley, reprising her role from the first *Vacation,* goes nowhere, and a sequence set at Hoover Dam feels like it belongs in another movie altogether. At first, the bit seems like it will be funny, as the cranky tour guide repeatedly uses the word "dam" in ways where "damn" would also be appropriate, e.g. referring to "the dam tour." But then Clark gets separated from the group and ends up dangling from the inside of the dam itself. He even swings on a power line, Tarzan-style. Such slapstick antics don't possess the satiric irreverence that is supposed to be a hallmark of the series. Fortunately, there are only a couple times when it goes this far off track.

What's admirable about *Vegas Vacation* – and what many people may have missed upon initial release – is that Chevy gets some genuine chances to dazzle here. Having Clark become blinded by the glitter of Vegas was fitting for the character; Clark is nothing if not blinded by perceived opportunities. This conceit leads to Chevy's best moment in the picture, in which the family meets for breakfast. Clark, itching for some action, gets up from the meal, walks into the casino to gamble, loses, and then comes back to finish eating. In the sequence, Chevy gets to play a sense of sinking despair as Clark feigns happiness for his family, then gradually drifts into utter misery. There is a deftness to his performance in this scene, in that he finds humor in the character's shifting emotions. Once again, Chevy proves underrated in being able to mine humor from common feelings.

Vegas Vacation was largely ignored at the box office. It earned only $36 million, making it the lowest-grossing entry in the series. The general consensus was that the movie's very existence was a cynical attempt to squeeze just a bit more cash out of an established franchise. What you probably don't know is that Chevy took the project very seriously and had a strong commitment to the material, according to director Stephen Kessler.

In an interview conducted exclusively for this book, Kessler, who did "a page-one rewrite" of the *Vegas Vacation* script with two other writers, discussed how the Griswolds came back to the big screen. "Chevy and Warner Brothers had money issues" over another film, he told me. The studio owed Chevy money and "they wanted a movie from him." Another *Vacation* sequel seemed like a logical idea. Warners brought in producer Jerry Weintraub, a well-known and much-liked figure around Las Vegas, to oversee the project. Here was a man who not only understood Vegas but could also get the production access to locations and assets. It helped that Weintraub "wanted a more reality-based" comedy.

Kessler's journey into the director's chair came through making an impression on both the producer and the star. "Warner Brothers had [National Lampoon executive] Matty Simmons as producer," Kessler says. "I met with him. He liked me. Then I met with Chevy. I told Chevy, 'A lot of your films aren't as funny as you were on TV. I could help you be as funny in your movies as you were on *Saturday Night Live.*" Over the course of a four-hour lunch, Chevy "really opened up to me" about his career frustrations. "I thought he was a really open, great, funny guy." Kessler had earned Chevy's trust and, with Simmons exiting the picture, the actor subsequently recommended him to Weintraub for the job.

The director and star put a lot of thought and planning into this fourth installment, much of it revolving around Chevy's desire to deliver comedy gold. Kessler told me that Chevy "had just finished shooting a movie in Canada" (presumed to be the 1995 Disney comedy *Man of the House,* which filmed in Vancouver) and didn't feel he was allowed to do much of his specialty work. Frustrated by the experience, he "didn't want to sleepwalk through this film. He really wanted to be funny." The two had long discussions about physical stuff Chevy could do, and scenes were built around the ideas they generated. Kessler specifically mentions the scene in which Clark and Cousin Eddie visit a buffet filled with disgusting food. Chevy "likes to do hand comedy," the director said, which led to the idea of doing one shot focused solely on his hands as he traverses the buffet, sampling and unsampling the items on display. Many scenes began as the seed of an idea, which the star then ran with. Kessler says Chevy would often tell him, "Let me do it. I know what to do with it." His ideas weren't limited to his own performance, though. A scene involving Cousin Eddie's son, who has his mouth pierced shut, was supposed to be just a visual gag. Kessler says it was Chevy's idea to have the kid mumble through his piercings. The sequence in the airplane bathroom was also born out of discussions about what Chevy could do. Having seen him improvise physical antics in restaurants for fun, Kessler was in tune with what his star could pull off.

Behind the camera, a conscious decision was made by the team to incorporate much of the real Las Vegas into the film and to shoot on location whenever possible. Kessler recalled childhood visits to Vegas where his father would gamble while he was left to roam around. The director therefore had a specific read on the city's unique energy. Weintraub, for his part, observed that adults don't want their families around while there, because they are a distraction. This informed Clark's decision to let Rusty and Audrey explore the city independently. A number of other things were done to build on the authenticity, including the fact that "the extras are real Vegas-y people" who were "pulled out of real shows." Kessler said of his background players: "It was great having that resource." Since he, Chevy, and Weintraub all wanted to film in Vegas as opposed to on a set, the producer greased wheels to get more genuine elements into the film. The Wayne Newton subplot, for example, was not in the original script; the singer was added because he's such a well-known Vegas fixture. Weintraub also secured the services of magicians Siegfried and Roy for a cameo in which they pull Clark onstage and make him disappear. The duo's act had never been filmed before.

I asked Kessler about Chevy's working relationships with Beverly D'Angelo and Randy Quaid. He told me that Quaid's role was "beefed up" significantly from the original script, and that this led to "a lot of improvising" with Chevy during his scenes. The two actors got along great on set, and "they loved playing off each other." Kessler adds that both Quaid and D'Angelo "approached the comedy as actors; they came from character." Quaid, in particular, "played it seriously," rather than playing it as though trying to be funny. This is an astute observation. With Chevy crafting material to play to his strengths, having two co-stars approach the primary supporting roles in a straightforward manner set up a strong dynamic that benefited the series as a whole.

Many ideas were generated on the way to bringing *Vegas Vacation* to the screen, but not all of them made it. During the rewriting process, Kessler envisioned a scene in which a distraught Clark went to the top of the 1,149-foot high

Stratosphere Hotel and considered jumping off. Weintraub put the kibosh on it. One can only wonder how this would have played out on screen. Audiences might not have liked seeing their beloved protagonist contemplating suicide, yet it undoubtedly would have brought a harder edge to the humor, not unlike the sequence in the original where Aunt Edna dies mid-trip and has her corpse strapped to the roof of the car.

That brings us to another very significant difference between *Vegas Vacation* and its predecessors. This one carries a tame PG rating, the lowest in the series. The original had an R rating, while the other two were PG-13. The shift to a PG indicated that the studio was intentionally trying to turn the series into something more family-friendly, which Kessler generally confirms. "When it came out, they weren't making R-rated comedies," he says. Considering its origins as a *National Lampoon* project, this was an odd way to go. Part of the appeal of *Vacation* was its subtle subversion of traditional family values, even as it was simultaneously embracing them. A PG rating suggested that the subversion would be missing. Still, Kessler is correct; it wasn't until a year later, with 1998's *There's Something About Mary,* that edgy R-rated comedies would come back into vogue.

Dismissed in its time, *Vegas Vacation* remains divisive. Many still view it as the bastard child of the franchise, while others maintain a fondness for the movie based on the elements that work. As of this writing, I am one of only four critics to have rated it "fresh" on Rotten Tomatoes. *Vegas Vacation* is certainly not the best film in the series, and it's certainly not perfect, but I do think it's better than *European Vacation* and contains some genuine laughs. I've probably seen the film four or five times over the years, and it never fails to amuse me. I asked Kessler – who says, "I wasn't even a *Vacation* fan. I was a Chevy Chase fan" - what he thinks of the picture. He told me that he hasn't watched it in years, but in an email exchange prior to our phone interview, he agreed with my assessment that it "has a lot of funny stuff in it." Kessler also noted that his film still pops up on television regularly, he still gets residual checks from it, and people still come up to him and quote lines from it.

Summary

Regardless of the quality of any individual installment, the *Vacation* series represents an important part of Chevy's career. Clark W. Griswold is a beloved character, one with whom the actor playing him will always be associated. It is safe to assume that a big reason why this match between performer and character is so effective is that Chevy identifies with Clark, which in turn makes him so empathetic. Although he had two previous marriages, Chevy found lasting happiness when he married his third wife, Jayni, in 1982, a year before *Vacation* was released. It was at this time that he became a devoted family man, much like his cinematic alter ego. By all accounts, he is a dedicated father to his three daughters, Cydney (born in 1983), Caley (born in 1985), and Emily (born in 1988). In interviews, he has always shown great pride when discussing his family and their importance to him.

This being the case, there's no doubt that Chevy "gets" Clark in a very personal way. Because they share a central trait, his performance gains authenticity. We sense that, more than anything else Chevy has ever done, this is the role that contains more of his own personality, his values, and his heart. He knows what it means to passionately love one's wife and adore one's children. This quality comes out on screen. Whereas a number of his roles have played to Chevy's strengths, Clark Griswold is the one that works at an even higher level. There are plenty of comedic possibilities in the character, yet also the opportunity to invest it with something deeper. This very quality is why Clark transcends the material; it's impossible not to love this guy.

Interesting Trivia:

The Griswold legacy has continued to live on. In 2010, Chevy and Beverly D'Angelo starred in an excruciatingly awful short film called *Hotel Hell Vacation.* This 14-minute video was actually an extended commercial for HomeAway, a company that specializes in vacation rentals. The two, along with several other cast members from the series, also starred in Old Navy ads that ran during the 2012 holiday season. The commercials paid homage to *Christmas Vacation.*

Christmas Vacation was a sequel that spawned its own sequel. *Christmas Vacation 2: Cousin Eddie's Island Adventure* was a laughless, virtually unwatchable 2003 TV movie that found the character trapped on a tropical island. Randy Quaid once again played the character, and Dana Barron reprised her role as Audrey.

Christmas Vacation is the only film in the series not to make use of Lindsay Buckingham's theme song "Holiday Road."

The films had varying performances at the box office. Here are their grosses, according to Box Office Mojo:

Vacation - $61 million

European Vacation - $49 million

Christmas Vacation - $71 million

Vegas Vacation - $36 million

It's important to note that, adjusted for inflation, the original would be the highest grossing of the films.

Critical approval rates varied as well.

Vacation – 94%

European Vacation - 38%

Christmas Vacation - 63%

Vegas Vacation - 13%

Deal of the Century

One of the things that often gets lost when looking at Chevy Chase's career is that he occasionally moved out of his safe zone. People largely remember the times when he played to his strengths but forget that he wasn't afraid to try something different. The problem is that, when he did take risks, the films were usually unsuccessful. Case in point: 1983's *Deal of the Century.*

In director William Friedkin's dark satire about the military-industrial complex, Chevy plays small-time arms dealer Eddie Muntz. We first meet him in a South American country, peddling rocket launchers to a couple of revolutionaries. As fate would have it, he meets Harold DeVoto (Wallace Shawn), who works for a major American defense contractor and is there to organize a lucrative deal. DeVoto has spent several weeks sitting in his dingy hotel room, waiting for "the call" to come. Depressed and despondent, he commits suicide moments before the phone rings. Opportunist that he is, Muntz answers the call and pretends to be DeVoto's replacement. He then finds himself negotiating the sale of a high-tech pilotless plane called the Peacemaker to some very shady people. Assisting him are his partner Ray (Gregory Hines), whose newfound religious beliefs are nudging him out of the arms business, and DeVoto's wife Catherine (Sigourney Weaver), who wants a cut of what would have been her husband's profits.

Deal of the Century is a movie that strives for a *Dr. Strangelove* level of satire, yet never comes close to achieving it. The screenplay, written by Marshall Brickman (*Risky Business*), tries to take on too much, and subsequently the film lacks a smooth flow. The bits of comedy are often interrupted for a moment of speechifying. There is a lengthy prologue in which Luckup – the company manufacturing the pilotless plane – develops an alarming advertising campaign aimed at instilling fear in the hearts of viewers. Later on, Muntz visits a well-connected arms merchant who gives him (and, by extension, us) a long, hard-to-follow lecture on the perceived future of the arms industry. In such sequences, it becomes clear that Brickman and Friedkin are heavily invested in mocking the military-industrial complex, but they forget to weave their message into the fabric of comedy, thereby rendering *Deal* a satire with few laughs. The movie eventually turns didactic, with a grand finale that sees Ray hijacking a jet fighter at an arms expo and helping the newly-disillusioned Muntz to destroy the Peacemaker prototype. In the end, Muntz gets out of the business altogether, working instead as a used car salesman.

I wasn't terribly fond of *Deal of the Century* when it originally came out. It simply wasn't funny like I expected a Chevy Chase movie to be. Revisiting it again 29 years later, I still don't find it funny – although I do recognize it as an admirably ambitious film. Brickman's script is never silly. It tries to address real issues and to engage the audience by pulling back the curtain on the arms industry. There are individual scenes, like the one in which Ray temporarily forgets his alleged pacifism and takes a flamethrower to another man's car in a fit of road rage, that suggest *Deal* has the right satiric spirit. Same goes for a sex scene in which stock footage of missiles is used to suggest intercourse. When the male in the pair is unable to perform, the footage switches to missiles crashing to the ground. That juxtaposition of sensuality and military strength is provocative, suggesting that people with vested interests in weaponry are almost fetishistic. As a whole, *Deal of the Century* never comes together; viewed for its individual elements, though, it is hard to deny that everyone involved was trying to do something amazing.

For Chevy personally, the movie was obviously an attempt to challenge himself. It was his first time working for an A-list director (Friedkin won an Oscar for *The French Connection* and was nominated for *The Exorcist*), and the subject matter was leagues beyond the slobs vs. snobs anarchy of *Caddyshack* or the screwball romance of *Foul Play*. Eddie Muntz is a darker, more cynical character than a Ty Webb or a Clark Griswold. He's a guy who does morally questionable things every single day, without necessarily feeling guilty about it. Chevy's performance is one of *Deal*'s highlights. Friedkin doesn't let him fall back on his usual mannerisms, either. There are no real bits of physical comedy, no pratfalls, no comic mugging. Instead, Chevy is asked to convincingly play sleazy and do a few wordy, elaborate sales pitches. In fact, with his fast-talking, highly-technical patter, Muntz feels more like a character custom-made for Dan Aykroyd. To his credit, Chevy pulls it off, displaying an edgier side to his comedy than people are used to.

Deal of the Century suffers from some other notable problems. The Sigourney Weaver character is woefully underdeveloped, and there's little justification for Ray's erratic behavior in the finale. The movie has a lot of good elements in place to satirize its subject, yet this is a case where a few significant flaws prevent it from reaching its potential. In the end, another Chevy Chase picture, *Spies Like Us*, would end up being a better, albeit sillier, take on similar subject matter.

Fletch / Fletch Lives

Fletch

It's not a fact that is immediately apparent, but several of Chevy's movies were based on books: *Funny Farm, Memoirs of an Invisible Man, Zoom,* and, of course, *Fletch*. The latter was released in May of 1985, giving Chevy his second most-beloved character, after Clark Griswold.

Fletch is based on the first in Gregory McDonald's outstanding and irreverent series of mystery novels. It tells the tale of Irwin Fletcher, an investigative reporter who writes under the pen name "Jane Doe." While pretending to be a bum as research for a story on the local drug trade, he is mistaken for an actual down-and-out drifter by millionaire Alan Stanwyk (Tim Matheson). Stanwyk claims to be dying of cancer and offers Fletch money to kill him and make it look like a robbery gone bad. The reporter plays along while simultaneously investigating Stanwyk. He discovers that the millionaire is actually healthy as can be, which means that the botched robbery scenario is actually a set-up for a complicated insurance scam. Using his wits, Fletch finds out what Stanwyk is up to, foils his plans, and even romances the guy's wife (Dana Wheeler-Nicholson).

In the books, Fletch was a fast-thinking reporter with a razor-sharp wit. He was always mentally one step ahead of everyone else. Consequently, much of their appeal rested in McDonald's clever wording, the way he crafted dialogue for the character that cut through the artifice of whomever/whatever he was investigating. There was no situation from which Fletch couldn't: 1.) talk his way out; or 2.) ascertain the information he needed to crack the case. Much of this quality is retained in the film, with screenwriter Andrew Bergman even keeping chunks of McDonald's dialogue intact.

When Chevy signed on to play the role, he added another element: Fletch became a master of disguise, repeatedly altering his appearance and/or providing phony names. (Among other monikers, he dubs himself Ted Nugent, Irving Babar, and, most famously, Dr. Rosenrosen.) Chevy has said in interviews that this started out as an improvisation and ended up becoming the cinematic Fletch's most well-known trait. The combination of McDonald's vision and Chevy's vision worked surprisingly well, giving him a well-developed character to play while still allowing him to bring something of his own invention.

The disguises and aliases are not the only things he brings to the movie. There is a sense of subversive exaggeration to the humor that only Chevy could pull off. When, for instance, Fletch puts on oversized glasses, sticks a Band-Aid on his nose, and calls himself "Mr. Poon," it's a ridiculous sight, but that isn't the only joke. The secondary joke is that everyone (us, Chevy, the film itself) knows it's ridiculous, while the other people in the story do not. Fletch virtually flaunts his manipulations in front of those he encounters, doing it with such supreme conviction as to become unassailable. The comic idea is that confidence is the ultimate salesman. Do things with conviction and you can fool anyone about anything. This becomes a key trait of Fletch; he gathers what he needs to nail Stanwyk by perfectly playing everyone from whom he needs information.

Fletch was a box office hit, earning $50 million at the box office, a very respectable sum for the time. Once it hit video and cable, however, it became a classic. This is obviously due, in part, to Chevy giving perhaps the most inspired performance of his career. Director Michael Ritchie allowed him to play with the material, to try ideas, to experiment. Chevy has always known what his gifts are, and having a director who trusted his instincts paid off magnificently. The memorable disguises/aliases and numerable quotable lines of dialogue ("Charge it to the Underhills." "I'm from the mattress police. There are no tags on these mattresses.") are hilarious, and he pulls them off with consummate skill. Simply put, he was "in the zone" on this picture.

If *Fletch* is one of Chevy's best movies – and I firmly believe it is - credit must also be given to the plot, which unfolds the mystery in a logical, coherent way. Unlike, say *Under the Rainbow* or *Modern Problems*, *Fletch* has a story that's actually worth following and which pays off in a satisfying manner. Ritchie and Bergman hewed very closely to McDonald's story. Unlike many book-to-film adaptations, they didn't feel a need to tinker with the basic source material. They kept the mystery intact, then used Chevy's ideas as an overlay. It should also be pointed out that, from a directorial standpoint, Ritchie knew when to indulge in absurdity and when to pull back into reality. A gifted cinematic satirist who previously directed *The Candidate, The Bad News Bears,* and *Smile*, Ritchie made three films with Chevy. The other two, *Fletch Lives* and *Cops & Robbersons,* were not on the same level quality-wise, but that's more a fault of the material. All in all, the two men were a good match, as their sensibilities melded nicely.

When looking at Chevy's entire filmography, you can see that his best films were the ones where his comic style was laid over top of a tight, controlled plot. (*Funny Farm*, which we'll get to in a bit, is another example.) His worst movies are the ones where he tried – or was asked to try – to use his comedy to prop up a flimsy plot. *Fletch* is Chevy at his best. On a personal level, I have to say that it is my favorite comedy of all time. Since seeing it opening weekend in 1985, I've watched *Fletch* at least a dozen times. It never fails to make me laugh hysterically, even though I know almost every single line by heart. Many others feel the same way; the movie maintains a devoted fan base.

Fletch Lives

It took four years for Irwin M. Fletcher to return to the big screen. *Fletch Lives,* released in 1989 and also directed by Michael Ritchie, made a huge mistake right off the bat: it opted for an original plot. Despite the fact that Gregory McDonald had a whole series of consistently terrific Fletch novels, they decided not to use any of them as the basis for the sequel. Andrew Bergman did not return as screenwriter, either. Instead, those duties went to Leon Capetanos, a writer whose previous credits included *The Gumball Rally, Moscow on the Hudson,* and *Down and Out in Beverly Hills.* While perhaps not possessing Bergman's distinct wittiness, Capetanos certainly had an impressive enough resume to suggest he could pull the job off. (When a writer's strike occurred shortly after production began, Ritchie took over rewriting duties.) Unfortunately, despite an undeniable number of laughs, the film's story tried to take on a subject that would have been admirable in another movie but was not really compatible with *Fletch.*

Fletch Lives begins with a short prologue in which Fletch, dressed in drag, foils a group of mobsters. (Having him in a dress takes the "master of disguise" concept to a too-absurd extreme.) Once back at his newspaper desk, he gets a call informing him that he has just inherited a Louisiana plantation. This causes him to promptly quit the paper and move south. It turns out that the plantation is run down. Undeterred, Fletch manages to bed the estate attorney who shows him the place, only to find her dead the next morning. His reporter instincts kick in and, suspecting foul play, he begins poking around to see who might have a grudge against her. What he discovers is that someone wants him off the plantation. A key suspect is a television evangelist, Jimmy Lee Farnsworth (R. Lee Ermey), who is scoffing up lots of local land in order to expand his theme park. Fletch infiltrates Farnsworth's operation, finding that the real culprit is an attorney named Hamilton "Ham" Johnson (the estimable Hal Holbrook). Ham has a grudge against Farnsworth and wants to dump toxic waste on the plantation's land to harm the theme park. He needed Fletch's land for his scheme, and figured that by framing the outsider for the murder of the attorney, he could scare Fletch away.

I saw *Fletch Lives* upon its release in 1989 and loved it. Not as much as the original, but enough to revisit it a number of times over the intervening years. Rewatching it for this book, I still found much of it funny, yet the flaws seemed to stand out more. Most likely, this is because the movie deals with something that has lost its relevance. When it was first released, *Fletch Lives* came on the heels of several real-life controversies and scandals related to televangelists. Jim Bakker, founder and host of a popular Christian TV show called *The PTL Club*, had engaged in a sexual encounter with a church secretary named Jessica Hahn. This brought his empire – which, like Jimmy Lee Farnsworth's, contained a theme park – crashing to the ground. Jimmy Swaggart, another well-known TV evangelist, was found to be cavorting with a prostitute, leading to his infamous "I have sinned" televised confession. Yet another evangelist, Peter Popoff, was exposed as a fraud when it was revealed that his "messages from God" were, in fact, transmitted to him via a hidden earpiece; he duped many followers into thinking that the Lord was speaking to him about them. (Again, shades of Farnsworth.) Today, preachers and faith healers like Bakker, Swaggart, and Popoff don't have nearly the ubiquity or relevance they had in the late '80s, which makes *Fletch Lives* feel a bit dated, whereas the first one is timeless.

It's easy to understand why a satirist like Michael Ritchie would salivate at the chance to take on televangelists, though; they were certainly ripe for targeting at the time. Chevy seemed to like the opportunity to mock them, too. At one point, Fletch disguises himself as "Claude Henry Smoot," and interrupts Farnsworth's TV broadcast with his own bit of faith healing. While the scene is too far-fetched, Chevy is in full force, accurately nailing the exaggerated cadence and mannerisms possessed by many preachers of the airwaves. It remains one of his most inspired bits of performance. Nonetheless, the movie at times strains under the weight of trying to support the subject, especially given that it's little more than a red herring to divert from the fact that Hamilton is the real culprit.

There's a second layer of satire going on simultaneously. *Fletch Lives* additionally skewers the South. Fletch's plantation comes with an African-American servant named Calculus Entropy (Cleavon Little), who talks like Uncle Remus. (He is eventually revealed to be an FBI agent independently investigating Farnsworth.) Jokes about slavery abound, and there's even one bit where Fletch makes a mockery of the KKK members rallying on his lawn. Because *Fletch* had a fantasy sequence – in which he imagines himself as a Los Angeles Laker – *Fletch Lives* has one, too. This time, it's a *Song of the South*-inspired musical number, complete with an animated bird and dog. This material holds up a little better than the televangelist stuff, although having them both squeezed together in the same movie robs it of the tight plotting that was crucial to *Fletch's* success. The sequel tends to meander, so eager is it to skewer both TV preachers and the South.

For whatever plot problems it may have, *Fletch Lives* still offers plenty of Chevy doing what he does best. In one of the funniest sequences, Fletch has to infiltrate a biker bar. He puts on the geekiest wardrobe possible, complete with fake mustache and glasses, then introduces himself to the burly bikers as "Ed Harley," the owner of Harley-Davidson motorcycles. As is often the case in Chevy's best moments, he is required here to be smarter than everyone else onscreen, and you actually believe Fletch is pulling this con off, so authoritatively does Chevy execute it. There are plenty of great ad-libs as well, from some of the throwaway aliases Chevy improvises (Nostradamus being one of them) to his trademark add-ons. While trying to extract information at a chemical plant, he explains away his surliness by claiming to have a hernia, adding, "I've been spitting up blood, pissing blood, bleeding." Not many people could come up with such a line, much less sell it. Then again, he's Chevy Chase and you're not.

Fletch Lives was substantially less popular than its predecessor, earning only $35 million at the box office and earning generally negative reviews. The *Fletch* film franchise came to a screeching halt. In the end, they would have been better off adapting another of McDonald's books. That would have grounded this sequel. Instead, the filmmakers attempted to mess with the formula. If I had to pick one single moment they got most wrong, it would be the one in which Fletch realizes the attorney in bed next to him is dead. Rather than being shocked or concerned, he cracks a one-liner about how the sex "wasn't *that* good." Anyone familiar with the first *Fletch* or any of the novels would know that Irwin M. Fletcher reserves his disdain for those who deserve it, and he has tons of empathy for innocent victims.

Interesting Trivia: There have been various attempts over the years to reboot the *Fletch* franchise. Most famously, director Kevin Smith wanted to do a film version of McDonald's prequel, *Fletch Won*, that was faithful to the spirit of the character on the page (i.e. no costumes or assumed names). Ben Affleck was his choice to play the role. Zach Braff and Ryan Reynolds have also had their names thrown around as candidates should Fletch ever return to the big screen. Perhaps wisely, Reynolds told *Entertainment Weekly* that he would never play the character because Chevy's portrayal is too iconic.

Spies Like Us

Although he left *Saturday Night Live* after only one season, Chevy was always associated with the show and maintained relationships with some of the other original cast members. The person he most often collaborated with was Dan Aykroyd. They would ultimately appear in several films together, the first of which was 1985's *Spies Like Us.* The movie had all the right pieces in place: a skilled comedy director, writers who knew how to craft a joke, and two stars who also happened to be old friends. Akyroyd penned the story with former *SCTV* star Dave Thomas and wrote the screenplay with the writing team of Lowell Ganz & Babaloo Mandel (*Splash, Night Shift).* John Landis (*Animal House, The Blues Brothers*) guided the ship from the director's chair, bringing his particular sensibility to the mix.

In *Spies Like Us,* the fictional Defense Intelligence Agency (DIA) needs two decoys to divert attention away from the fact that they are planning to hijack a Soviet missile launcher. By stealing it and launching a missile, the US government can test a new satellite defense system designed to shoot down anything the Soviet Union might aim in America's direction. The DIA recruits two hapless government employees to be the unwitting decoys. Austin Milbarge (played by Aykroyd) is a codebreaker for the Pentagon who yearns to get out of his dingy basement office and do something big. Emmett Fitz-Hume (played by Chevy) is the son of an envoy who thinks his status will allow him to coast. The two men meet after cheating on the

Foreign Service exam. Sensing that they are both clueless and expendable, the DIA sends them through some haphazard training and then ships them off to Pakistan. After enduring a series of comic mishaps, Milbarge and Fitz-Hume get wise to the fact that they are decoys and are not happy. They are, however, effective. The launcher is hijacked and a missile is fired. Unfortunately, the defense system doesn't work, meaning the U.S. has launched a Soviet missile at itself. It is the potential start of World War III. Milbarge knows they must spring into action, so he and Fitz-Hume suddenly become real spies, using some technical know-how to recall the missile before it can hit.

Spies Like Us has a very interesting comic approach. It plays on '80s-era nuclear fears, yet does so in the guise of a tribute to the old Bing Crosby/Bob Hope *Road to...* pictures. The film intentionally has the form of that series, with the characters ambling along on a comical trek filled with wacky misadventures, meeting a beautiful woman (in this case played by Aykroyd's wife, Donna Dixon) who becomes something of a sidekick, and eventually reaching a happy ending. Nowhere is the formula more obviously alluded to than in a sequence set in the desert in which Bob Hope himself wanders through the frame chasing an errant golf ball.

It's not hard to understand why Chevy would be drawn to this material. First and foremost, it gave him the opportunity to reunite with old pal Aykroyd. Having worked together in the past, the two men fundamentally understood each other's rhythms. The importance of that in comedy cannot be understated. A good on-screen partnership requires knowing how to the set the other guy up for the joke. Chevy and Aykroyd knew how to do this. Interestingly, neither of them plays the straight man. Both portray characters who are a bit dim, albeit for different reasons. Milbarge is desperate to climb the career ladder, which makes him short-sighted. Fitz-Hume is a con artist, a guy who thinks he can bluff his way out of anything. One of the movie's funniest scenes finds them taking that Foreign Service exam. Milbarge hasn't had time to study, and Fitz-Hume arrives with his arm in a fake cast, the answers to the test tucked away inside. The latter begins cheating; the former sees him and, sensing an opportunity, helps. The scene ends with them getting caught but refusing to believe it. Fitz-Hume fakes a panic attack, and Milbarge fakes guiding him through it. This is one of many scenes that allow both actors to strut their stuff.

A very intriguing thing about the picture is that it successfully mixes the physical humor that is obviously in Chevy's wheelhouse with the more cerebral humor that Aykroyd does so well. When Fitz-Hume and Milbarge are put into a G-force simulator, they emerge with their faces stuck in a contorted position. That's classic Chevy. Later on, the pair, pretending to be doctors, are introduced to a group of real doctors, leading to them all addressing one another by their title. (Doctor. *Doctor.* Doctor. *Doctor.* Doctor. *Doctor.*) This is vintage Aykroyd. Watching the two meld their personal styles is certainly one of the great pleasures of *Spies Like Us.*

They may be front and center, but one should not discount the impact of John Landis on the movie. The director's clean, unfussy style suits the material well. Landis often uses the camera as an impartial observer. He doesn't like to trick up his shots too much. Given the frequent absurdity of the onscreen antics, he doesn't need to; the straightforward style helps keep everything in balance. Landis also adds a sub-layer of humor. As a treat for film buffs, he casts other directors in supporting roles. Among them: Frank Oz, Terry Gilliam, Ray Harryhausen, Martin Brest, Sam Raimi, and Joel Coen. The movie's premise involves covert operations, and Landis stages a covert operation of his own.

Chevy sometimes worked with skilled comedy directors (Landis, Michael Ritchie, Harold Ramis) and sometimes with those who were less talented (Ken Shapiro, Steve Rash). He obviously thrived the most when working with the good ones. Throughout his career, Landis has shown an understanding of how to make every comic actor's skill set shine through, while still working within the confines of the overall film. He not only successfully worked with Chevy, but also Aykroyd, John Belushi, Eddie Murphy, Steve Martin, and even Don Rickles. With *Spies Like Us,* the director set a structure that allowed both of his lead actors to bring their A-game.

As such, there are plenty of big laughs in the picture. Where *Spies* runs into a bit of trouble is in the third act. At this point, needing to resolve a rather dramatic crisis in which the world is nearly annihilated, the plot starts to take itself a bit too seriously, causing a decrease in the number of comic moments. This is actually a typical problem with Aykroyd-penned screenplays; *Ghostbusters* and *The Blues Brothers* also had decreases in jokes during their respective finales. (*Ghostbusters* at least had the highly humorous sight of the Stay-Puft Marshmallow Man, which made the problem a little less noticeable.) *Spies Like Us* gets a touch draggy in the last twenty minutes, as Milbarge and Fitz-Hume race to recall the missiles that are heading straight toward the United States. What began as a joyously goofy buddy comedy abruptly turns into something of an action flick.

Spies Like Us holds up well, though, despite its Reagan-era Cold War themes being outdated. Chevy and Aykroyd are funny individually and as a team, and they are surrounded by supporting players who elevate their game. While it doesn't reach the classic status of *Vacation* or *Fletch*, it is nevertheless a solid entry in Chevy's career, one that was a box office success in its day and remains popular with his fans.

Three Amigos

Of all the movies in Chevy's filmography, *Three Amigos* is the one that has had the most significant change of status. When it was released in December 1986, the comedy – which teamed Chevy with fellow comedians Steve Martin and Martin Short – was expected to be a blockbuster. Felled by bad reviews and lackluster word of mouth, it grossed a disappointing $39 million at the box office. (For comparison, *Spies Like Us* earned $60 million.) When Johnny Carson asked film critic Roger Ebert what the worst movie of the holiday season was, Ebert famously answered that it was *Three Amigos* – despite the fact that Chevy was seated right next to him on the couch. In spite of these things, the picture evolved into a significant cult hit more than a decade after its release. Its showbiz-spoofing storyline was a little ahead of the curve in 1986. Such self-knowing humor wouldn't become fashionable until the mid-'90s. Today, the movie has a devoted legion of fans, in addition to a sparkling anniversary edition Blu-Ray, the release of which was met with great excitement.

Chevy, Martin, and Short play, respectively, Dusty Bottoms, Lucky Day, and Ned Nederlander. They are former silent movie actors who starred in a series of Westerns before getting fired by the studio chief (Joe Mantegna). When the small Mexican village of Santa Pico is terrorized by a brutal bandit named El Guapo, one of the locals, Carmen (Patrice Martinez), writes to the Amigos and asks for help. They misinterpret her plea as an invitation to make a paid personal appearance. Once in Santa Pico, they expect to put on a show, scare off El Guapo, and collect a nice paycheck. It doesn't take long for them to realize that the situation in which they find themselves is very, very real. Initially, the Amigos intend to ride off into the sunset (or, at least, back to Hollywood) but they're ultimately so moved by the town's plight that they take on El Guapo and his henchmen for real.

Looked at today, it's not hard to see why *Three Amigos* didn't make a splash upon the initial release. While it never breaks the fourth wall, the film does try to form a knowing bond with the audience. The spoofing of actors, stardom, and cinematic genres was not something pop culture saw a whole lot back then. It wasn't until the early '90s that self-referential or "meta" humor became hip. Jerry Seinfeld famously created a TV series about "nothing," and the original *Scream* movie rewarded audiences for their knowledge of horror movie cliches. *Three Amigos* was released in an era where pictures like *Short Circuit, The Money Pit,* and *Crocodile Dundee* were indicative of the big screen comedy culture.

A bigger problem for Chevy was that the humor really wasn't his own. Steve Martin wrote the screenplay (with help from Lorne Michaels and musician Randy Newman), and the film bears all the hallmarks of his conceptual style of comedy. Much like the Martin-penned *L.A. Story* and *The Jerk, Three Amigos* isn't afraid to go off on weird little tangents. For example, the Amigos make their way through the desert in search of a "singing bush." After a long, arduous journey, they stumble upon a solitary shrub, with high-pitched musical vocals emanating from it. "Do you think that's the singing bush?" one of them asks. Martin has always had a brilliant ability to pull off this sort of bizarre, borderline surreal humor. It's not Chevy's forte, though. While he does manage to work in a few bits of his own physical comedy and detached irony, there simply aren't enough opportunities for him to do so. (Martin Short, too, finds himself looking for chances to engage in his patented manic physicality.) It's great to see the three comedians sharing screen space, but the movie itself is never as uproarious as fans probably expected in

1986. I recall seeing the film as soon as it opened and working hard to convince myself that I was enjoying it. Parts of it made me laugh, although other pictures that year accomplished the task more thoroughly.

Now, divorced from the sky-high expectations of the time, *Three Amigos* is quite funny. Chevy, Martin, and Short have the kind of chemistry that only comes from authentic friendship. They display a generosity with one another, with each of them expertly setting up the other two guys rather than trying to hog the best moments for themselves. In fact, the best scenes in the film are the ones where they're doing something together, such as reciting the "Amigo Salute" or cluelessly singing "My Little Buttercup" to a bar full of hostile gunslingers. A sequence in which the guys put on their show and are then confused as to why El Guapo and his men haven't been scared off is also very funny. Each comedian registers the surprise in his own way, creating a collectively hilarious end result. The bizarreness of the humor is yet another selling point. During a campfire number, various animals join the Amigos in song. And who can forget the Invisible Swordsman, who is slain, creating an indentation in the ground as he drops?

Three Amigos was Chevy's second consecutive film with director John Landis, who went through some difficulty getting his work to the screen. After he turned the movie over, executives at Orion Pictures decided to cut certain sections out, including a lengthy opening sequence (seen on the Blu-Ray) with the Amigos getting ready for work in a mansion and then traversing a studio lot, as various types of pictures are being filmed behind them. A supporting performance from comedian Sam Kinison as a bloodthirsty mountain man was gone, too. Future *Nanny* star Fran Drescher's part was all but excised, as well. It's a fair assumption that the studio didn't "get" *Three Amigos* or, at the very least, wanted to turn it into something other than the weird little meta-comedy it obviously is.

It's not a stretch to say that *Three Amigos* influenced other movies. The 1999 comedy *Galaxy Quest* co-opted its premise quite shamelessly. In the picture, Tim Allen fronts a band of washed-up actors who had once been the stars of a popular science-fiction television program. The leader of an alien race, who believes them to be real space adventurers, enlists their help in fighting an intergalactic warlord trying to extinguish his people. It's up to the hapless actors to save the day for real. Sound familiar, like *Three Amigos* in space? Ben Stiller's brilliant 2008 comedy *Tropic Thunder* similarly made fun of thespian vanity by thrusting a bunch of actors, who think they're making a war movie, into a real war. Here again, performers are placed in a situation that requires them to use their natural talents to survive, and possibly even to help defend innocent people.

Three Amigos may not have made the financial splash many expected – *Police Academy 3: Back in Training, Legal Eagles,* and even *The Golden Child* were more popular comedies at the box office that year – but its stature has grown, and it is now recognized as a funny, ahead-of-its-time piece of meta goofiness.

Funny Farm

By the late '80s, Chevy was ready to take a new form of control over his career. He set up his own production company, Cornelius Productions (after his real first name), to create vehicles in which he could star. The first Cornelius picture was 1988's *Funny Farm,* an adaptation of Jay Cronley's novel. In addition to securing the rights to a well-regarded book, the project added further prestige by bringing on George Roy Hill to direct. Hill was an Oscar-winning filmmaker, having helmed everything from *Butch Cassidy and the Sundance Kid* and *The Sting* to *Slap Shot* and *The World According to Garp.* It was clear that Chevy wanted to produce something amazing – and he did.

In the opening scene, we meet New York sports writer Andy Farmer (played by Chevy) as he is roasted by some of his poker buddies. Andy has decided to leave the city and move into an idyllic country home in Redbud, Vermont with his wife Elizabeth (portrayed by Madolyn Smith). Here, he will finally get around to writing his Great American Novel. Things do not go according to plan. Initially, the troubles are minor. The movers get lost and accidentally destroy a covered bridge in the process. The phone isn't hooked up. The alcoholic mailman tosses letters across the Farmers' front lawn. Then things get really dire. While gardening, Elizabeth finds a corpse buried in the backyard. Andy gets writers block. The couple's attempts to make friends spectacularly backfire, to the point where people begin to hate them. Eventually they realize that everything is a disaster. Their marriage on the verge of falling apart, Andy and Elizabeth decide to sell their home. They attend a town hall meeting, offering to pay cash to any local citizen observed performing an act of kindness in front of potential buyers. The greedy townsfolk take the offer overboard, suddenly turning Redbud into something right out of a Norman Rockwell painting. (They *really* want to get rid of the Farmers.) This "performance" has the opposite effect. Andy and Elizabeth decide that they love each other and still want to live in Redbud. They pay everyone off as a gesture of goodwill and happily settle into their new life.

Funny Farm is an adept skewering of idealism and the fantasy of perfection. Andy Farmer has a specific vision of what life in Redbud will be like, and that vision leaves no room for anything unexpected. Piece by piece, his vision falls apart, as imperfection repeatedly creeps in. In the end, to achieve the perfection he desperately craves, Andy literally has to buy it. That's a sharp satiric concept.

It's also one that might sound a bit familiar. *Funny Farm* and *National Lampoon's Vacation* – arguably Chevy's two "best" films – both share the same general premise. In each case, an idealistic character strives for perfection, only to have his fantasy disassembled before him, leading to frustration, anguish, and the need to take extreme measures to make things right. (The *Vacation* sequels operate under this same premise too, although not quite as strongly as the original.) Chevy must have responded to this idea at some level, either consciously or unconsciously. It certainly plays to his strengths as a comic actor, giving him multiple opportunities to portray increasingly frazzled despair.

One has to wonder why this theme recurred throughout his career – and traces of it can be found in some of his other, later movies, as well. At the risk of playing armchair psychiatrist, it's not a stretch to assume that he must have felt like Clark Griswold and Andy Farmer at points during his life. After hitting it big on *SNL*, Chevy seemed to be charmed, as though the world was at his feet. Life was not as smooth as it may have seemed from the outside looking in, though. Before finally finding long-term happiness with wife Jayni, Chevy went through two failed marriages. He battled an addiction to painkillers, and has acknowledged having had problems with alcohol and cocaine. By his own admission and to his own regret, he left *SNL* too early. And then there were some of the high-profile box office flops. What could have been a charmed life turned out to be full of unexpected pitfalls. But in the end, like Andy and Clark, Chevy managed to find happiness. His third marriage worked. He kicked the drugs and booze. He survived his flops. Most importantly, he embraced his role as a father. The road may not have been as simple or ideal as it could have been, but when all was said and done, he triumphed, just like the characters he played.

His likely identification with the material allowed Chevy to perform at his absolute peak in *Funny Farm*. Giving a reined-in performance, free from the mugging his detractors often accused him of, he plays outrageous moments in a realistic, down-to-earth way. One need only look at the scene in which Andy excitedly fishes in his backyard pond. Thinking he's snagged a big one, he pulls in his rod, only to discover that he has actually hooked a snake. Chevy turns the scenario into a kind of dance, as Andy jumps, squirms, and generally tries to fend off the slithering creature. It is not Chevy being goofy, it's Chevy doing a realistic, but ever-so-slightly exaggerated take on what someone in this predicament would really do.

Funny Farm had a smart script from writer Jeffrey Boam (*Indiana Jones and the Last Crusade, Lethal Weapon 2* and *3*), and the great George Roy Hill made sure to emphasize the humanity underneath the broad comedy. As such, Chevy gave a performance unlike any he'd given before. His finest moment comes about mid-way through. Andy, having beaten his writer's block to finally bang out a draft of his novel, rents a motel room and insists Elizabeth sit and read it while he watches. (She thinks they're going out for a romantic evening.) As she reads, eagerness fills Andy's face. The scene soon cuts to a short time later. Elizabeth tells Andy she hates what he wrote. He can't understand it. He goes through the stages of grief, denying that it's bad, bargaining that parts of it surely *must* have been good, and finally accepting that his wife may be right. He throws the manuscript into the fire. Realizing it's his only copy, he then quickly reaches in to pull it out. Chevy gets to play a wide range of emotions in this sequence, as the character goes from giddy anticipation to outright crushing defeat. The writing, direction, and performances all blend perfectly, resulting in a scene that makes you laugh while still feeling tons of sympathy for poor old Andy.

This sort of magic is found throughout *Funny Farm.* Some moments are just funny, such as the one in which Andy breaks the record for eating the most "lamb fries" at the local diner, only to discover that he has devoured sheep testicles. Others find humor in pain, as when Andy learns that Elizabeth has secretly written – and sold – a children's book about a hapless squirrel who bears a suspicious resemblance to him. One scene after another in this movie hits the comedy bullseye.

Working with a solid script and an A-list director gave Chevy the opportunity to hit new heights as an actor. Not just as a comedian, but as a genuine actor. Critics, most notably Gene Siskel and Roger Ebert, raved about both the film and his performance in it. Amazingly, *Funny Farm* was not a hit, grossing just $25 million at the U.S. box office. Some of that may have been due to its competition. Also opening on June 3, 1998 was the Tom Hanks comedy *Big,* which became a smash hit. Oddly, though, *Funny Farm* never really caught on through home video, either. It is a movie that absolutely deserves to be mentioned whenever discussing Chevy's classics. Consistently hilarious and thoroughly winning, *Funny Farm* is long overdue for recognition as one of the best big screen comedies of the 1980s.

Nothing But Trouble

One of Chevy's highest-profile bombs was released on February 15, 1991. *Nothing But Trouble* had, in fact, been trouble almost from the beginning. The movie marked the directorial debut of Dan Aykroyd, who also wrote the screenplay. Chevy later went on to say that he did the film as "a favor" to Aykroyd. Whether he ever saw any potential in the material is difficult to say, but his pseduo-dismissal of it is predictable. His experience on set reportedly wasn't entirely pleasant, as he and co-star Demi Moore are said to have intensely disliked one another. The film also had a bumpy road to the screen; the title was changed from the original *Valkenvania*, and it sat on the shelf at Warner Brothers for several months after they bumped it from its original 1990 release slot. Opening in over 1,600 theaters with lackluster promotion, *Nothing But Trouble* earned just $8 million on a $40 million budget and received overwhelmingly awful reviews.

A couple critics did give it good notices, one of whom wrote the book you are now reading.

Nothing But Trouble is the story of financial publisher Chris Thorne (Chevy) who agrees to drive his sexy new neighbor Diane Lightson (Moore) to Atlantic City. Tagging along for the ride are two of Chris's Brazilian clients, Renalda and Fausto Squiriniszu (Taylor Negron and Bertila Damas). Chris wants to stay on the highway, but everyone else convinces him to take a more scenic route. They end up driving through a small Pennsylvania town called Valkenvania, where mine fires burn beneath the ground. Chris accidentally runs a stop sign and is pulled over by the local constable, Dennis (John Candy). Everyone is forced to appear before the local judge, the 106-year-old Alvin Valkenheiser (Aykroyd, under heavy makeup), who lives and works in a ramshackle old house in the middle of what appears to be the world's largest junkyard. The judge turns out to have massive contempt for bankers (or anyone he *thinks* is a banker), so he sentences Chris and company to death. That's right – the death penalty for a traffic violation.

Renalda and Fausto manage to escape, while Chris and Diane are stuck inside Valkenheiser's trick house, which comes with trap doors, moving walls, and sliding boards. Out in the backyard sits a roller coaster that, when it reaches the end, tosses its riders into a contraption known as "Mr. Bonestripper." This grisly little device rips the flesh off anyone unlucky enough to enter it and spits their bones out a chute in the back. Valkenheiser eventually agrees to let Chris live, so long as the "banker" will marry his mute granddaughter Eldona (also played by Candy, in drag). Chris reluctantly agrees, but then pisses off the judge and ends up being sent through Mr. Bonestripper. Fortunately, the machine malfunctions and he survives, just in time to rescue Diane from the clutches of two hideously deformed creatures, Bobo (Aykroyd again) and Debbull (John Daveikis), who toil away in the junkyard. They get away, heading to Pennsylvania's Capital building to report the sinister goings-on in Valkenvania. Police raid the judge's home, but it is revealed to be a trap; they all know and love the judge, and have conspired to return Chris and Diane so that they may face their sentence. Just then, the underground mine fires start blowing through the surface, and our couple manages to escape.

Given what I've just described, it's little wonder that *Nothing But Trouble* was discarded by the studio and ignored by the public. The movie is dark and weird. *Seriously* weird. I recall catching the first Saturday showing of it on opening weekend. The theater was only about a quarter full, with no one laughing except for me. And I was laughing hysterically.

I've always had a firm opinion on this movie, which was reinforced after watching it recently for the fifth or sixth time. It is not a bad movie so much as it is a movie aimed at people with a very specific and twisted sense of humor. *Nothing But Trouble* mines humor from the most unlikely and disturbing of subjects: capital punishment, psychological torture, human deformity, semi-incestual family relationships, etc. Not everyone is inclined to see humor in these things. It all begins with the premise. If you think the idea of someone getting the death penalty for running a stop sign is funny, you'll probably like the film. If not, you probably won't. Aykroyd makes no apologies for pursuing the strangest, most outlandish ideas he has, from Valkenheiser's penis-resembling nose to the sequence in which a group of drug-addled travelers are sent through the gears of Mr. Bonestripper. Some of the comedy value for me rests in the picture's willingness to play such things for laughs, but I also think it mixes silliness with taboo quite well. Aykroyd creates a creepy/funny vibe, like a jaunt through an amusement park haunted house. He also throws in intentional contradictions. At one point, Valkenheiser drops Chris and friends through a trap door in the floor, which leads to a dingy, scary basement pit. Yet they land on a cushion of rubber dog toys that squeak playfully upon impact.

Another highlight comes when a group of rap musicians is pulled over by Valkenheiser's cop niece, Miss Purdah (Valri Bromfield). The judge insists the musicians, portrayed by real rap group Digital Underground, prove their occupation. They set up their instruments in his chambers. A handcuffed Chris looks on in disbelief as they perform the movie's theme, "Same Song" (which makes another appearance over the end credits). Valkenheiser, who has a keyboard built into his desk, joins in for a mean solo before dismissing all charges against the group. The scene may be a little *apropos* of nothing, although it does provide a bit of levity amidst the otherwise grim proceedings.

Over the years, I've found a number of other people who adore *Nothing But Trouble* as I do. Again, you have to possess a specifically warped sense of humor to see the value in it. Some of my personal fondness for the film may have something to do with the fact that I live in Pennsylvania and have been through towns exactly like the one presented here. Aykroyd drew on real-life places for his fictional burg. One of them was Centralia, Pennsylvania, whose citizens largely abandoned it because of an underground mine fire that has burned since 1962. I recall going through Centralia as a teenager. Smoke billowed up from the ground. Not a soul was in sight. It was undeniably spooky. The fact that towns like Valkenvania really exist gives the movie a compelling foundation.

All this is not to say that *Nothing But Trouble* is perfect, or even great. A few jokes fall flat, the supporting characters could be developed more, and the Chevy/Demi chemistry is understandably non-existent. Perhaps most egregiously, the ending reeks of having been reshot. Thinking he is safe, Chris turns on the TV news and sees a report about the destruction at Valkenvania. The reporter interviews a "survivor," who is, in fact, the judge. He still has Chris's driver's license and vows to come looking for him in New York. The movie ends with Chris jumping up from his couch and running through the wall of his apartment, leaving a human-shaped hole in it. This final shot is handled sloppily. It feels like something ripped out of a Looney Tunes short, which is wildly out of place with the film's overall tone, and we only hear Chris crash through the wall, rather than see him do it. It really feels like there must have been some other, darker ending that didn't work and was replaced with something stupider.

Considered from a distance, Chevy's assertion that he took the role of Chris Thorne as a favor to Aykroyd appears legit. Nothing about the film or the character seems natural to him. With the exception of this one project, Chevy never worked "dark." His movies could be edgy or politically incorrect, but there was never anything about his comic persona that seemed interested in pursuing the sort of odious subject matter that permeates *Nothing But Trouble.* Even more tellingly, the picture requires him to largely play straight-man. Chevy, usually the comic center of any film he's in, is forced to react to all the weirdness going on around him. It must have been disconcerting for him to have to play against every natural instinct he has. A few attempts seem to have been made to give him more to do. There is a lot of ADR (automated dialogue replacement) in

Chevy's scenes, indicating that someone realized he wasn't getting to be funny and suggested he ad-lib a few quips.

His performance is not bad, though, in light of the material's poor fit. During the scene in which Chris rides the roller coaster on the way to Mr. Bonestripper, Chevy exudes a genuine sense of terror. Chris begins begging God to save him. He gets his wish, which provides the scene with a tension-defusing conclusion as Chris looks around, realizes he hasn't been torn to shreds and, with a sigh of relief, says, "Thank you, Lord" before walking off. The wedding sequence offers his biggest chance to be funny. When Chris is forced to say "I do" to marrying Eldona, Chevy makes the choice to have his voice break up in terror. What comes out is not so much "I do" as a streak of panicked gibberish. This is one of the biggest laughs in the whole thing.

Nothing But Trouble continues to suffer from a bad reputation, despite a small cult audience, and the studio gives no indication of having pride in it. As of this writing in early 2013, Warner Brothers has never released a proper version of the movie on video. A DVD exists, but it is a cropped pan-and-scan version. There is currently no way to see *NBT* in its proper aspect ratio, nor can you catch it in high-definition. Hopefully, this will change someday. In an interview a few years back. Aykroyd took full blame for *Nothing But Trouble*'s poor reception. I hope he doesn't regret making it, though. Yes, it may have bombed badly, and yes, the majority of critics may have torn it apart Mr. Bonstripper-style. But you know what? Aykroyd had the guts to make something deliberately odd, unpredictable, and risky. He should be commended for that.

Memoirs of an Invisible Man

There's no denying that Chevy was one of the biggest stars of the 1980s. However, by the beginning of the '90s, a comedy shift was taking place, and a new generation of comedians was rising to prominence, replacing the previous generation in terms of popularity. Nowhere was this made more evident than in the February 28, 1992 release of *Memoirs of an Invisible Man.* The movie was supposed to be a big hit. It had ambitious source material (H.F. Saint's acclaimed novel), groundbreaking-for-the-time special effects, and an unexpected but intriguing collaboration between Chevy and famed horror director John Carpenter (*Halloween, The Thing*). On the surface, it seemed like *Memoirs* couldn't lose. However, a mere two weeks before its release, a little movie called *Wayne's World* had come out and captured the nation's attention. A surprise box office phenomenon, *Wayne's World* turned *Saturday Night Live* players Mike Myers and Dana Carvey into full-fledged stars, spent five consecutive weeks at the top of the box office charts, and launched a plethora of catchphrases. *Memoirs of an Invisible Man* looked like old hat in comparison. Making matters worse, the film was trounced in its opening weekend, earning just $4.6 million, whereas *Wayne's World,* then in its *third* weekend, pulled in $9.6 million. Chevy's days as a bankable leading man were officially over.

Saint's book was ripe for a screen adaptation, although it required some pruning. It's the story of a man who becomes invisible, with the bulk of the novel dedicated to describing how he survives, how he manages to earn money despite not being able to go to work, how he hides out in his private club because it's one of the few places that provides comfort, etc. It is actually kind of a sad book, in that the story mines issues of loneliness and isolation. Saint made invisibility seem like a nightmare.

Carpenter's film is more of a comedy/adventure. Chevy plays Nick Halloway, a yuppie stock analyst who doesn't take much of anything seriously. Then he meets Alice (Daryl Hannah). They have a strong, instant connection. Suddenly, he can imagine settling down. As happened to Clark Griswold and Andy Farmer, Nick's vision of perfection is ruined by an unforeseen calamity. While attending a meeting at Magnascopic Laboratories, a lab worker spills a cup of coffee onto a computer keyboard, setting off a system-wide meltdown. (It was a common cliché of the time to have something bad happen by spilling liquid on a keyboard. Of course, anyone who knows anything about computers will tell you this leads only to a wet keyboard.) Nick, hungover from the night before, takes a nap in a sauna, completely oblivious to the fact that the building has been evacuated. Some kind of molecular craziness takes place, leaving large chunks of the building – and Nick – invisible.

Sam Neill plays David Jenkins, a CIA agent who wants to bring Nick in for "examination." Nick is wisely mistrustful of Jenkins, who, in fact, wants to use the invisible man as a secret agent. Nick continually eludes his nemesis, eventually hiding in a beach house owned by his friend George (Michael McKean). When George and some friends, including Alice, show up for a weekend getaway, he moves to the abandoned house next door. He then makes contact with Alice and reveals his secret. She agrees to help him. Together, they launch a plan to get rid of Jenkins by threatening to deliver a videotape proving Nick's invisibility to the press. The film ends atop a building under construction. Jenkins lunges at what he mistakenly thinks is Nick, only to fall to his death. Now safe from the threat, Nick and Alice follow through on their plan to move to Switzerland, "where a guy can get away with wearing a ski mask all year round."

Memoirs of an Invisible Man was originally supposed to be directed by Ivan Reitman, the comedy master behind *Stripes* and *Ghostbusters.* He reportedly wanted to direct a goofy invisibility comedy, whereas Chevy was interested in segueing into slightly more substantive roles. Consequently, Reitman left the project and Carpenter stepped in. It was definitely a work-for-hire job for the filmmaker, who typically created and wrote his own projects. *Memoirs* was developed by Chevy as the second (and, it would turn out, final) Cornelius production. The screenplay was written by Oscar winner William Goldman (*Butch Cassidy and the Sundance Kid),* Dana Olsen, and Robert Collector.

The collaboration between Chevy and Carpenter is most certainly an odd one. The former gentleman starred mainly in broad comedies, while the latter made his name with horror and science-fiction fare, much of it containing graphic violence. Even though Chevy wanted to make something less broad, he is said to have disagreed with his director on the tone. He wanted it to still have *some* comedy, whereas Carpenter was reportedly more interested in making it darker. Critics seemed to sense this, as the reviews were not very good. *Entertainment Weekly* film critic Owen Gleiberman wrote, "There's every indication that director John Carpenter was trying for more than another rinky-dink Chevy Chase comedy. Except for the effects, though, *Memoirs of an Invisible Man* comes disappointingly close to being just that."

Such reviews miss a crucial point: *Memoirs* is actually really good. The movie's sensibility works, with the comedy serving to illustrate the difficulties of being invisible. In one of the most memorable sequences, Nick eats some food and, seeing it digest in his transparent stomach, promptly pukes. (The audience sees the partially digested food coming up through an invisible throat and out an invisible mouth.) Another cool moment finds Nick smoking a cigarette, as we witness the smoke filling his lungs. Such bits are funny, yet they also highlight the idea that invisibility can be betrayed. That, in turn, makes Jenkins' pursuit of Nick even more suspenseful. Nick is more vulnerable than he initially thinks.

Some of the comedy is just pure Chevy, though. Unaccustomed to his new status, Nick at one point runs into something and does a pratfall. Minutes later, when Jenkins, sensing the invisible man is nearby, asks what his name is, Nick responds, "Harvey" - a tribute to the Jimmy Stewart movie about an invisible rabbit. It is a classic deadpan Chevy delivery.

Carpenter, meanwhile, delivers a taut pace, playing up the idea that, even unseen, Nick is in danger of being tagged by Jenkins. Mid-way through the film, Nick sneaks into his adversary's office to gather intelligence. After squatting in a corner all day, he lets out a barely audible sigh as he adjusts his position. Jenkins hears it and immediately knows his prey is in the room. You'd think it would be easy for an invisible man to get away, yet Carpenter shows how Jenkins is wily enough to compensate for a seeming disadvantage. There are tense bits like this throughout the film, expertly mixed in with the comedy.

The visual effects remain impressive, despite the fact that such things have improved significantly since 1992. From the opening shot, in which the invisible Nick chews a piece of gum, to the touching scene were Nick and Alice kiss in the rain, the water revealing his outline to her, the effects create a convincing illusion. Nothing in Chevy's resume had been anywhere near this effects-heavy, which made his presence in the film a pleasant novelty.

Because of its blend of comedy, suspense, and ambitious visuals, *Memoirs of an Invisible Man* is one of Chevy's most interesting projects. He really tried to do something outside the box here. Nick Halloway is also an uncommon role for him. While there are a few distinctly Chevy-esque lines and physical bits, the character is unhappy and lonely. He wants his normal life back. His malady takes a toll on him. Chevy is unafraid of mining this emotional turmoil. He must have learned from his mistakes on *Modern Problems*, as this time he portrays a miserable character much more sympathetically. As with *Deal of the Century*, though, this attempt to mine more depth as an actor was lost amidst poor reaction to the film. Chevy's detractors often claimed – unfairly, I might add – that he only ever did variations on his own persona in movies. *Memoirs* is proof that this accusation isn't true. Once again, the range of his talent becomes clearer. Yes, he can be silly and goofy; he can also project sorrow and detachment.

I saw *Memoirs of an Invisible Man* as soon as it was released and enjoyed it very much. Over the years, I've watched it several more times. Seeing it again now, I find that my opinion hasn't changed. Buoyed by strong supporting performances from Sam Neill and Daryl Hannah, the movie deserves more recognition than it has received. No, it's not perfect, but it is a genuinely compelling work that offers both laughs and thrills.

Cops & Robbersons

Coming off the flops of *Nothing But Trouble* and *Memoirs of an Invisible Man,* Chevy attempted to return to his wheelhouse by playing a very Clark Griswold-esque character in 1994's *Cops & Robbersons.* The movie re-teamed him with his *Fletch/Fletch Lives* director, Michael Ritchie. The central joke here is that Chevy does his patented broad comedy alongside co-star Jack Palance, who does the same grumpy guy schtick that won him an Oscar for *City Slickers.* Unfortunately, Palance didn't have nearly the same chemistry with Chevy that he did with Billy Crystal. The mismatched pairing felt...mismatched.

Cops & Robbersons represents the kind of "high concept" comedy Hollywood was churning out in the mid-'90s. Chevy plays Norman Robberson, a suburban dad obsessed with cop shows on TV. He has an encyclopedic knowledge of them, often throwing quotes around in normal conversation. When a mob hitman named Osborn (Robert Davi) moves in next door, a real cop, Jake Stone (Palance), and his young partner, Tony Moore (David Barry Gray), check into the Robberson residence to stake out the guy's home. Norman, of course, wants to help, much to the irritation of Jake. As the investigation goes on, he inserts himself into it more and more, even going so far as to talk his way into Osborn's house so he can sneak around for clues. Meanwhile, the crotchety Jake has to learn how to integrate himself into a family. Tony, on the other hand, has no such problem; in a really creepy subplot, he romances Norman's teen daughter. (All together now: *Ewwww!*) When all is said and done,

Norman gets the chance to help take down a bad guy, while Jake softens his tough-guy exterior a little bit.

Once again, we find Chevy playing a husband and father. It should be reiterated that some of the appeal of this role certainly must have been identification, as he himself was a devoted family man by this point in his life. Norman Robberson is a lite version of Clark Griswold – just as enthusiastic, just as clueless, but obsessed with cops rather than Walley World. The role must have felt like a natural to him.

Look closely and you will also see a touch of that recurring theme involving the search for perfection. The Robbersons are not entirely a happy family. Daughter Cindy (Fay Masterson) is rebellious, son Kevin (Jason James Richter) craves a father figure he can relate to, and five-year-old Billy (Miko Hughes) dresses up like a vampire. Wife Helen (Dianne Wiest) tries to hold everything together as best she can. Norman feels the weight of his unhappy family. He just wants everyone to be normal. He also wants the chance to play the hero for once in his life. Much of the movie is devoted to Norman's comic frustration that things cannot just be simple. We have already established that part of this theme is that the character eventually does get what he wants, after enduring numerous trials. By the time the end credits roll, Norman has had the chance to help nab a big time criminal, thereby earning the respect of his family. He is now "cool" in their eyes. The Robbersons will be a more functional family from this point on.

Sadly, the screenplay – by Bernie Somers, in his first and only writing credit – is lackluster. Norman's cop show obsession never feels authentic; instead, it feels more like a screenwriter's contrivance. When Chevy holds a gun and does his best imitation of Robert DeNiro in *Taxi Driver*, it seems designed to be a joke, rather than something that springs from Norman's mentality. The vast majority of what transpires in *Cops & Robbersons* is equally problematic. Credibility is often stretched, especially as it pertains to the gullibility of the bad guy. No matter what asinine thing Norman does, Osborn never catches on to the fact that he's under surveillance. Instead, he believes every outrageous lie Norman and/or Jake (who poses as an uncle at one point) tells him. Only in the third act, when manufactured drama is required to come into play to create a finale, does he wise up and show his true menace.

This is one of the last movies Michael Ritchie directed, and it suggests that he'd lost his feel for satire. The mid-'90s were a time when the Fox TV show *Cops* was a major cultural phenomenon, as was *America's Most Wanted*. Presumably, the idea of real-life law enforcement cases being televised as entertainment contained plenty of satiric possibilities. *Cops & Robbersons* finds just about none of them. It exists merely as a gimmick: Goofy Dad clashes with No-Nonsense Cop.

This means that Chevy has very little of substance to work with. He seems a bit bored in the role, almost as though he knows there are lost opportunities everywhere. (In fact, he told biographer Rena Fruchter that the movie was "a piece of crap I did for the money.") On occasion, he gets to cut loose. Another fine example of hand comedy comes when Norman attempts to scrape the cream cheese off a bagel and ends up getting the whole thing stuck to his fingers. That's a funny bit. Most of the humor is not of that variety. A typical gag involves Norman swinging from a rope, with the intention of crashing through the bad guy's front window, but smashing into the side of the house instead.

I awarded *Cops & Robbersons* three stars in my original 1994 review. My pull quote on Rotten Tomatoes is still there; I call it "a vastly underrated Chevy Chase comedy." Years later, I can no longer make that claim. It's not a terrible movie, yet it *is* terribly bland. (I'd give it two stars today.) Still, *Cops & Robbersons* was not the lowest point of Chevy's career in the '90s. Shortly after production on the film wrapped, he went on to do his notoriously maligned late night talk show. That the film came out after the talk show was canceled only added insult to injury.

Man of the House

When comedians' careers begin to cool, there is always a safe haven: family movies. These features often have low budgets – or at least lower than most productions on a studio slate – and benefit from having a recognizable face that can be plastered on ads. This is especially important in the international market, which relies on the presence of "name" stars to drive foreign sales. With a series of recent box office disappointments behind him, Chevy went through a period, as many comic actors do, where he found work in films aimed at kids. It started with *Man of the House* and went on to include *Snow Day* and *Zoom,* which we'll get to shortly.

Man of the House (released in 1995) was actually a vehicle for Jonathan Taylor Thomas, a young actor who had gained a rabid, mostly female, teen following thanks to his role on the hit TV show *Home Improvement*. His face appeared regularly in teen magazines, although he was never able to parlay that into a successful screen career. (*Tom and Huck, The Adventures of Pinocchio* and *I'll Be Home for Christmas,* all released after *Man of the House,* were also flops.) This Disney production put Taylor Thomas alongside some notable adult co-stars.

The movie is about a young boy named Ben Archer, who lives with his single mother Sandy (Farrah Fawcett). Ben is very protective. He doesn't want his mom to get hurt, nor does he want her in a relationship, as that would mean he'd have to share her. Sandy falls in love with attorney Jack Sturgess (that would be

Chevy) and desperately wants Ben to like him. He doesn't. In fact, Ben does everything he can think of to drive Jack away. Jack, trying to be a good boyfriend, bends over backwards to please Ben. Unable to get rid of his nemesis, Ben asks Jack to do something he's sure will be unpalatable: join the "Indian Guides," a scouting group where everyone dresses up in Native American garb and learns to throw tomahawks, among other things. Jack does indeed hate the experience, especially after Ben gives him the Native American name "Squatting Dog." At the same time, a mobster that Jack put away (not the same one from *Cops & Robbersons*) is plotting to kill Jack. The criminal and his cronies make their move during an Indian Guides camping trip, giving Ben and the other kids a chance to use the skills they've learned to defeat the would-be killers and save Jack. Do I even need to say that going through this ordeal draws Jack and Ben closer?

You may be thinking the same thing I was when I saw *Man of the House* theatrically and again for this book: Why does a movie about a guy trying to bond with his girlfriend's son need a subplot about a mafioso? Is this really necessary? With a few momentary exceptions - such as the scene in which the mobster severs the brakes on Jack's car, sending him careening out of control – the first two-thirds focus mostly on Jack trying to earn Ben's trust, and Ben refusing to give it. There's nothing spectacular about it, but it does contain a certain emotionality that would probably resonate with any kid or adult who'd found themselves forced into a new family unit. The last third focuses on this ridiculous and surprisingly violent crime element - involving dynamite, an abandoned mine, and a bees nest - that undoes any relatable quality the movie may have had up to that point. Instead of going for an ending that truly has something worthwhile to say about blended families, it instead resorts to mindless slapstick and unearned sentimentality. What a depressing message to send to young people: you can learn to get along with your parent's new significant other, so long as you get to have a life-threatening adventure first.

As suggested by *Vegas Vacation* director Stephen Kessler earlier, Chevy was apparently not too happy making *Man of the House*. He isn't given the chance to do much that's funny. The character is more a victim of comic circumstances than an instigator of them. The situations are supposed to be funny, and some of the supporting players are supposed to be funny, but Jack Sturgess is not especially funny at all. One or two concessions are made, yet they fail woefully. During a scene in which Jack wants to make Ben laugh, he and another dad attempt to assemble a tent, banging each other with poles and bashing one another in the head with mallets. Of course, whacking somebody with a hammer would lead to a concussion and possibly even death, but the movie has no time for little annoyances like logic. Such bits – which also include a music montage of the Indian Guides dancing – are out of place anyway. They're too goofy to mesh with the blended family plot, and the crime element is already out of left field.

While his role is not inherently comic, Chevy does deliver a nice turn. Here again, several recurring factors from his career reappear. Like many of his characters, Jack is a family man, eager to make a nice life with Sandy and Ben. Chevy's own devotion to family comes through in his sensitive performance. Also popping up is the theme of unsuccessfully looking for perfection. Jack envisions a wonderful, happy life with his girlfriend and her son, only to find a hostile child and a vengeful gangster keeping him from achieving it, for a while at least. *Man of the House* is not the best or fullest representation of this recurring theme, although it's impossible to deny that it is present.

On the whole, the movie is pleasant but unremarkable. Had it toned down the occasional attempts at slapstick comedy and scrapped the crime subplot altogether, *Man of the House* could have been a nice, earnest little family film – the kind of thing parents planning to remarry might have shown their children to open up lines of communication. Regrettably, the screenplay, by director James Orr and writing partner Jim Cruickshank, doesn't trust the value of its premise. The film feels the need to manufacture a bogus reason for Ben and Jack to bond. Perhaps the writers simply weren't skilled enough to know how to earn this honestly.

Snow Day/Zoom

Snow Day

After *Man of the House,* Chevy made *Vegas Vacation,* and then returned to family films, some of which he had supporting roles in, others of which featured only a brief cameo. The most notable of these are the 2000 Nickelodeon production *Snow Day* and the 2006 Tim Allen vehicle *Zoom.*

As its title suggests, *Snow Day* is the story of a scenic New York town that gets hit with a blizzard, which dumps several feet of snow on the ground. The town's children are ecstatic, since the inclement weather means a day off from school. Chevy plays Tom Brandston, the father of two of these children. He's also a meteorologist who is forced to wear funny costumes during his weather broadcasts as a means of upping the low ratings. Tom's rival (played by John Schneider) is a slick, handsome guy with big ratings and little actual knowledge of weather patterns. The plot, such as it is, largely follows a bunch of kids launching an assault on "Snow Plow Man" (Chris Elliott), a nasty public servant with rotten teeth whose mission is to plow all the snow so the children will have to go back to school, rather than receive a second day off.

Snow Day is really bottom-of-the-barrel entertainment, as it condescends even to its youthful audience. There are so many familiar elements. Tom has an awkward-but-hopelessly-romantic son named Hal. He pines for Claire, the pretty, popular girl who doesn't know he exists. Claire has the requisite obnoxious jock boyfriend who lives to torment Hal. Then there's Hal's best female friend, who harbors a secret crush on him. There's also an overbearing school principal, a mother who's too busy with her job to pay attention to her kids, and a fat child who farts whenever a punchline is needed. It is almost as though *Snow Day* was written by a computer program that had analyzed every other film in the genre.

It is hard to imagine Chevy being in love with this material. Here's a man who satirized presidents and politics, who subverted traditional family values for laughs, who made movies that dealt (overtly or subtextually) with issues like bigotry and American military might. Now he's stuck in a dumb kiddie comedy with jokes about yellow snow and farting. This was a paycheck movie all the way, not that you can fault an actor for needing a paycheck. What's worse, though, is that *Snow Day* isn't just stupid, it's also irresponsible. The movie portrays anti-social behavior that most parents would not want their kids to emulate. At one point, the children steal a snow plow (leading me to wonder how an 11-year-old knows how to drive a stick shift, but that's a whole other matter) and run down another child with it, in what's supposed to be an example of "getting what you deserve."

Snow Day marks the second movie in which Chevy takes an out-of-control sled ride, the first, naturally, being *Christmas Vacation*. The difference is that, this time, he's dressed as a snowman when it happens. Stuff like this is typical of the movie. Everything in it has been done before, and done much better. Chevy does what he can, but the screenplay is so far beneath him that it's an uphill battle.

Zoom

Somewhat better, but still nothing extraordinary, is *Zoom,* a movie that tries – and fails – to be a teenage *X-Men*. Tim Allen stars as Jack Shepard, a guy who had once been a superhero known as Captain Zoom. He headed up a group of heroes, all of whom were killed in action by a villain called Concussion. Following that tragedy, Jack hung up his cape and disappeared. The movie finds him being called back into action by Larraby (Rip Torn), the military leader in charge of America's superhero program. When intelligence suggests that Concussion is returning to Earth via a time portal, Larraby sends two of his scientists, the geeky Marsha Holloway (Courteney Cox) and the bumbling Dr. Grant (Chevy), to retrieve Jack.

The retired superhero (who has since lost his powers) is forced to return to headquarters and train an assemblage of kids – ages 6 to 17 – each of whom has some sort of unfocused mutant ability. One has super-strength, another can move things with her mind, a third can turn invisible, and so on. Jack doesn't want to train the kids, but he later learns that the only alternative is for Larraby to douse them with a toxic chemical that will artificially cause their powers to develop. Since Jack was once jolted with the chemical and therefore knows the hazards firsthand, he reluctantly helps the kids get ready to battle Concussion.

Zoom is a movie almost totally bereft of originality. Just look at the powers possessed by the children. These things have been used over and over again in comic books and movies. The film would have been vastly improved by giving them more appropriate powers. How about a little boy whose whining can shatter glass? Or a moody teenager capable of shooting looks that literally kill? There's a lot of room for ingenuity, but the movie doesn't seem interested in doing the legwork. Granted, it was based on Jason Lethcoe's novel *Zoom's Academy*, but screen adaptations "improve" on literary source material all the time.

The cheapness of the visual effects and sets is matched only by the dullness of the plot. For at least half the running time, it's unclear exactly who or what Concussion is, so the threat never feels real. Good superhero movies need good villains, and *Zoom* doesn't have one. No wonder the final battle is so short and that the film is padded with at least half a dozen musical training montages. There's even a forced "we're all a family" message that is completely unearned, given that there's nothing in the characterizations to warrant it.

Whereas *Snow Day* is maddening, *Zoom* is at least watchable, largely due to Chevy. He gives a highly amusing supporting performance as Dr. Grant. Sporting pancake makeup, a bad comb-over, and clothing that *might* have been stylish in the early '70s, Chevy at least tries to do something interesting, unlike Tim Allen who, as usual, plays Tim Allen. He appears invigorated here, as though he's eager to introduce his distinct physical humor to younger audiences – something he wasn't allowed to do in *Man of the House* or *Snow Day.* The movie's idea of wit, however, is to have a character whose power is to blow snot bubbles out of his nose. One of them pops, spraying Dr. Grant in the face. Later, Grant gets sprayed in the face by a skunk.

As you can tell, *Zoom* didn't try very hard. Why challenge the imagination of young audience members when you can give them cheap snot jokes instead?

Chevy's forays into kiddie cinema did him no favors. *Snow Day* was a minor hit, earning $60 million, although that was on the strength of its incessant promotion on Nickelodeon. *Zoom* flopped massively, making just $11 million. There were other kid-flicks around this time (*Karate Dog, Goose on the Loose, Jack and the Beanstalk*). None of them helped his career in any way. In fact, they gave him some of the least inspired material in his entire filmography.

Interesting Trivia: Both *Snow Day* and *Zoom* make extensive use of Smash Mouth songs on their soundtracks. Then again, so did many movies in the mid- to late-'90s.

Ellie Parker

By the year 2000, Chevy's career was largely dead in the water. He'd left Hollywood, frustrated by the lack of quality scripts coming his way. Occasionally, he'd take a small part in a film just for the paycheck. (See: *Snow Day*) In 2004, *Entertainment Weekly* magazine did what was basically a "Where Are They Now?" piece on him, which documented a humiliating Comedy Central roast (none of his friends showed up, leaving a bunch of second-tier comedians to rip him apart, despite not knowing him) and the failure of his late night talk show. But the article also hinted at the possibility of a third act to his career. Chevy confessed to taking some meetings in Hollywood, only to find that a younger generation of executives and filmmakers, who had grown up on his movies, were interested in working with him. Whereas members of his own generation only saw the flops, the new Hollywood players saw a comedy icon, and they began offering him work.

One such person was Scott Coffey. You may not recognize the name, but you'd undoubtedly recognize his face. Coffey was himself an actor who had appeared in *Ferris Bueller's Day Off, Some Kind of Wonderful, Wayne's World 2,* and David Lynch's *Mulholland Drive*, among many other films. During the filming of *Mulholland Drive,* Coffey became friendly with the female lead, a then little-known actress named Naomi

Watts. The two began shooting a short film about a struggling actress dealing with show business rejection. They decided to expand it into a feature film, spending four years working on it as time permitted. *Ellie Parker* was a very independent production; often, it was just Coffey, the actors, and a cameraman shooting on digital video. And for a crucial role, Coffey landed Chevy Chase.

For Chevy, this was the start of a new phase in his career. Suddenly, he was making a cool little indie, with a hip young director and an actress who was quickly establishing herself as one of the most respected talents in the business. Perhaps it's no surprise that, in one seven-minute scene, he knocked it right out of the park.

Ellie Parker is like an actor's version of *Curb Your Enthusiasm*, i.e. an examination of pain, embarrassment, and crippling neuroses. The film follows Watts' title character as she hops from one audition to another, desperately trying to please casting directors and filmmakers who won't specifically state what they're looking for. She participates in acting classes that don't seem to actually teach anything, tentatively dates a cinematographer (played by Coffey), and routinely questions her own talent.

In a key scene about two-thirds of the way through, Ellie seeks the council of her agent, Dennis Swartzbaum (Chevy). Initially, she unloads her woes on him, announcing an intention to quit the business altogether. But then the tables turn, with Dennis admitting that his wife left him and that he's had plastic surgery. Ellie ends up comforting *him*.

In his role as Dennis, Chevy gets to do something very interesting. He starts off as a voice of authority, encouraging Ellie to stick with it, while offering sage, compassionate advice on the harsh realities of making it as an actor. As the sequence progresses, though, we see a softer, more vulnerable man sitting behind that big agent's desk. The role of Dennis is completely un-Chevy-like. There's none of the physical comedy he's known for, none of the off-the-cuff wisecracks. It's simply a good actor playing a vital role, and bringing important depth to it in the process. In fact, Chevy is so good in the role, you practically want to see a spinoff movie about his character.

In the *Ellie Parker* DVD commentary, Coffey says that, for some reason, he imagined Chevy in the role while writing and, in fact, ended up writing the part specifically for him. He then sent the script and an assemblage of footage that had already been shot with Watts. Chevy responded strongly to it. (No surprise, since he himself had been forced to deal with humiliation and rejection in his career.) Coffey also states that Chevy was eager to do what he perceived as an edgy art film. Working without a big crew "really freed him." The DVD also contains a longer version of the scene between Ellie and Dennis, in addition to outtakes and behind-the-scenes footage of Chevy at work. These bonus materials support Coffey's claim that it was a joyous shoot. Chevy seems fully committed to the work. He does indeed seem free.

Ellie Parker, with its highly personal examination of thespian angst, is probably a bit too "inside baseball" for general audiences, but for anyone with a decent understanding of the movie biz, it is a funny and insightful film. Naomi Watts again proves her fearlessness as an actor, allowing herself to be unglamorous in portraying this frazzled, insecure woman. And Chevy turns in a showstopping scene, showing that, while his career may have been dormant, his talent was as blazing as ever.

Funny Money

I'd seen every movie Chevy had ever been the main star of before writing this book. If there was one I dreaded revisiting, it was *Funny Money*. Released by a small, independent distributor in four theaters for one week on January 26, 2007 – where it earned a total box office haul of $2,844 – *Funny Money* was an exercise in torture when I first viewed it. Not even my intense love of Chevy could make sitting through this movie tolerable. The film is a madcap farce, based on a well-received British play by Ray Cooney. Farces of this nature work beautifully onstage, where you can see the actors performing lightning-fast physical comedy right in front of your eyes, in real time. Film tends to suck all the air out of them, though. There's editing, and changing camera angles, and comical music laid over the scenes. All these things create an artificial pace, as opposed to one that's organic. For these and other reasons, I unequivocally hated this film just as much the second time as the first.

Chevy plays Henry Perkins, an executive at a wax fruit company. One night on his way home from work, he accidentally switches identical-looking briefcases with a man on the subway and ends up in possession of $5 million of mafia cash. Figuring the man on the subway will show up to his workplace to look for him, Henry plots to flee to Barcelona with his wife Carol (Penelope Ann Miller). She, however, has planned an elaborate birthday party for him. The first guests to arrive are friends Vic (Christopher McDonald) and Gina (Alex Meneses). Then two separate detectives show up, independent of one another, when Henry's briefcase and wallet are found in the river. One is Genero (Armand Assante), the other Slater (Kevin Sussman). Henry, trying to prevent both law enforcement officials from discovering that he is in possession of stolen money, sets in motion an increasingly intricate series of lies and assumed identities, eventually dragging his wife and friends into the mix as well.

Once the farcical elements start to ramp up, *Funny Money* becomes extremely labored and irritating. Every line of dialogue uttered by Henry, Carol, Vic, and Gina is stammered and stuttered, as they struggle to remember their lies or make up new ones. We are meant to laugh at their desperate attempts to keep everything straight and spontaneously invent an excuse for some new wrinkle the cops point out. The problem is, none of it is actually funny. The script is poorly written, as it awkwardly tries to "open up" the theatrical nature of the piece by tossing in scenes set outside the Perkins apartment. (The ones with the mobsters trying to track Henry down are particularly painful.) The direction by Leslie Greif is leaden, failing to provide the lightness of tone that *might* have made the material work. As for the acting...well, better that we should call it over-acting instead. Miller is shrill, Assante seems like he wandered in from another movie altogether, and Guy Torrey, playing a cab driver who gets mixed up in all the nonsense, proves to be a genuinely annoying presence. It's like he's trying to do stand-up comedy in the middle of a movie.

The sole bright spot is Chevy himself. It's no wonder he wanted to make *Funny Money.* Farces are all about timing and precision – things he excels at. Whereas most of the other cast members seem clueless as to how the material should be pulled off, Chevy at least understands the mechanics of it. However, he's not able to bring everyone else (or the script) up to his level, so you end up with one solid performance in a mire of contrivances and poorly executed moments of physical comedy. Still, after the flops that had plagued his career by this point, taking the lead in an independently produced, adult-themed farce must have been appealing. (It's worth noting that *Funny Money*, with its numerous sexual jokes, is one of Chevy's few R-rated pictures.)

You can almost feel him trying to take charge of his career, tackling a project that, on the surface, seemed tailor-made to his comedic strengths.

The gamble didn't pay off. *Funny Money* didn't do much better overseas than it did in the States. Its total global haul was just a touch over $31,000. Considering the production went all the way to Bucharest in an effort to lower the budget to only a few million, that's a pretty pathetic sum. Even made on a tight budget, the movie couldn't begin to achieve anything approximating success.

Funny Money would turn out to be, at least as of this writing, Chevy's final leading role in a motion picture.

Odds and Ends

Throughout his career, Chevy occasionally took supporting parts or made cameos. Here's a brief look at his brief performances.

*

Sesame Street Presents: Follow That Bird **(1985)** – Chevy plays a TV newscaster in this feature-length movie inspired by the beloved TV show. When Big Bird flees Sesame Street, it sets off an adventure to find him. Chevy's comedy contribution is to humorously mispronounce Sesame Street, calling it "Se-*same* Street." *Follow That Bird* loses some steam in its second half, but is overall a cute film for kids.

The Couch Trip **(1988)** – This Michael Ritchie comedy tells the tale of an escaped mental patient (played by Dan Aykroyd) who poses as a licensed psychiatrist and fills in for a radio shrink (Charles Grodin) taking a leave of absence after a mental breakdown. Chevy appears as "Condom Dad" in a fake TV spot. In it, a father goes through his son's sock drawer and, finding a box of rubbers, expresses his pride that sonny boy is using the "right" brand. It's a quick cameo, apropos of nothing, but still very funny. Imagine an old *SNL* commercial parody plopped into the middle of a movie. *The Couch Trip* doesn't nail its intended satire, showing a penchant for sentimentality and easy resolutions, but it does have some decent performances and a few honest laughs.

L.A. Story **(1991)** – Steve Martin's brilliantly quirky ode to love and Los Angeles is filled with weirdly inventive moments. (How it never achieved status as a comedy classic is beyond me.) Chevy appears for exactly 30 seconds, playing a movie star frustrated that he can't get a good table in a swank new restaurant. He's not given anything especially funny to do; the bit is more about having an actual star bring his celebrity status to the scene.

Hero **(1992)** – Once again, Chevy had an opportunity to work with an A-list director; in this case, it was Stephen Frears, the man who helmed *My Beautiful Laundrette* and *The Grifters* (and, later, *High Fidelity* and *The Queen*). Dustin Hoffman plays a louse who goes against his nature and saves people after a plane crash. When a homeless man (Andy Garcia) takes credit for the act of heroism, Hoffman sets out to expose him. Chevy plays the head honcho at a TV news program whose star reporter (Geena Davis) has fallen for the imposter. In a most unusual, but completely satisfying, choice, he opted to play his character as almost a stereotype of an old-timey news editor. Dressed in suspenders and perpetually yelling, he's like J. Jonah Jameson from the Spider-Man comics come to life. This was clearly an opportunity to try something highly respectable, to appear in a film from an acclaimed director, written by a heralded screenwriter (Oscar-nominated *Unforgiven* scribe David Webb Peoples), and starring one of the greatest actors ever (Hoffman). Chevy's cameo is uncredited and amounts to maybe five or so minutes of screen time, but it's a glorious five minutes. He gets to do another bit of "hand comedy" during a scene in which his character awkwardly attempts to arrange a bouquet of flowers. *Hero* also reunited him with Davis (who'd played his secretary in *Fletch*) and Stephen Tobolowsky, who was his co-star in *Memoirs of an Invisible Man*. *Hero* is not remembered as anyone's best work. It is an ambitious film, yet also one that has some difficulty living up to its promise. Not bad, but not the awards magnet it was clearly conceived to be, either.

Last Action Hero (1993) – Chevy appears for literally three seconds in this Arnold Schwarzenegger action movie. Talking to Damon Wayans at a Hollywood event, he is knocked out of the way by Arnie.

Dirty Work (1998) – Chevy has a small part as a doctor in this Bob Saget-directed(!) attempt to squeeze the off-kilter humor of star Norm McDonald into movie form. McDonald plays a guy who launches a revenge-for-hire business with his brother (Artie Lange). Chevy's bumbling Dr. Farthing (farting – get it?) is a surgeon who tells McDonald that his father (Jack Warden) will die without a heart transplant, then asks for $50,000 to bump the old man up on the list. We learn that Farthing owes money to a bookie; every time we see him throughout the movie, he's sporting another new injury. I found *Dirty Work* moderately amusing when I reviewed it in 1998, but today, the seams really show. McDonald can be a funny guy, but he relies on the same punchlines again and again. Some of them are questionable in their humor content. How many times can he try to milk a laugh by calling a woman a "filthy whore"? Chevy has some fun with his cameo, but there's nothing particularly notable about the film.

Orange County (2002) – Director Jake Kasdan asked Chevy to appear as Principal Harbert in this coming-of-age comedy about a high school student (Colin Hanks) trying to get into college so he can become a successful writer. Chevy's cameo amounts to less than a minute of screen time, during which he cracks a joke about Britney Spears. While not especially substantive, Chevy's appearance indicated that a new generation of filmmakers was ready to bring him back into the fold. *Orange County* didn't find a whole lot of box office love, but it's a smart, sweet, funny little film that is worth seeking out.

***Our Italian Husband* (2004)** – This Italian romantic comedy is about a young woman who makes her way to America in order to find her missing husband, only to learn that he has a second family on our shores. Chevy plays Paul Parmesan, a shady home shopping channel guru, peddling merchandise that could generously be called crap. Paul briefly employs the woman, trying to steal a new type of "bio-fiber" she invented in the process. Aside from the fact that spoofing home shopping networks was about a decade out of date in 2004, *Our Italian Husband* suffers from a weak script, even weaker direction, and co-star Brooke Shields (as the second wife) delivering the most atrocious New Yawk accent in the history of cinema. Chevy looks lost and hopeless here.

***Karate Dog* (2004)** – For the *second* time in his career, Chevy provided the voice of a murder-solving dog in a family-oriented caper comedy. Let that soak in for a minute. *Karate Dog*, as you might expect, features a dog doing karate, allowing for the two-millionth cinematic reference to the "bullet time" effect popularized by *The Matrix.* The highlight (or is that lowlight?) of the movie is a climactic battle between the karate dog and the villain, played by Jon Voight. (Voight finally found a film to be more embarrassed by than his *Baby Geniuses* flicks.) It's a measure of how cheap *Karate Dog* is that the CGI canine used for the fighting sequences looks nothing like the canine used in the live action scenes. On the plus side, this picture is so wretched that it makes *Oh! Heavenly Dog* look reasonably watchable in comparison.

***Bad Meat* (2004)** – This is as horrible a movie as you will ever see. *Bad Meat* is the story of two losers who work at a meat packing plant and decide to kidnap a U.S. Congressman (Chevy) for ransom. The film was written and directed by Scott Dikkers, the former editor-in-chief of the very funny satire website, The Onion. It's shocking that someone who produced so much witty material for a website like that could create a movie so ugly and devoid of laughter. *Bad Meat* is the kind of picture that thinks it's funny to make all its characters as physically unattractive as possible. Chevy, therefore, is required to wear a bad wig and false teeth. His congressman dies early on, leading to several sequences where the other characters drag his body around, *Weekend at Bernie's*-style. Later, he accidentally falls into a meat grinder and is turned into bologna, which hits supermarket shelves. Please, don't ever watch this movie. I'm sure Chevy would make the same request.

Goose on the Loose (2006) – This low-budget kids' comedy casts Chevy as a mean cook, who steals a talking goose from an 11-year-old boy whose mother just died. (You have no idea how much I wish that I was just making that up.) Various slapstick hijinks ensue. Need I say more? Hopefully Chevy was paid well.

Doogal (2006) – Harvey Weinstein bought a British/French animated film called *The Magic Roundabout,* edited it heavily, had a bunch of needless pop culture references dubbed in, and released it in the U.S. under the title *Doogal.* A roster of stars provided new voices for the characters, including Chevy, who portrayed a train. It is typical of the humor that he is required, upon introduction, to say, "I'm a train and you're not." This, obviously, is a reference to his famous *SNL* catchphrase. The plot concerns a dog who has to prevent a guy whose torso rests on a giant spring from stealing some magic diamonds. *The Magic Roundabout* was well regarded in countries where it was released; *Doogal* was rightly panned in America.

Stay Cool (2009) – As he did in *Orange County*, Chevy again plays a high school principal in this comedy about a struggling writer (Mark Polish) who goes back to his hometown to give a commencement speech. Once there, all his adolescent neuroses come flooding back. He also makes a stab at dating the girl (Winona Ryder) he never had the guts to ask out at the time. That premise could make for a clever twist on the coming-of-age comedy, but *Stay Cool* doesn't do anything with it, instead relying on obvious jokes and stereotypes, including the main character's flamboyantly gay best friend (Sean Astin). Chevy gets to do some distinctly Chevy-esque bits as the wacky principal. We first see him coming up from under a desk (for reasons humorously unknown), and in several scenes, for no obvious reason, he sports a Band-Aid on his nose. Beyond his antics, there's not much funny to be found here.

Hot Tub Time Machine (2010) – Chevy has a cameo in this comedy about four hapless buddies who accidentally return to 1986 via a hot tub that is also a time machine (hence the title). He plays a mysterious maintenance man who explains that a Russian energy drink is the thing that allows the device to work. The casting of Chevy in a small role is one of the movie's many nods to the '80s, and a nice little touch. Personally, I find the humor in *Hot Tub Time Machine* hit-or-miss, but Chevy is clearly in on the joke, earning laughs with his limited screen time. Still, it was kind of sad to see him at a point in his career where he was cast primarily for nostalgia.

Jack and the Beanstalk (2010) – Yet another misguided foray into children's entertainment. This live-action take on the classic fairy tale features a lot of recognizable faces surrounded by fake, obvious sets. Chevy plays a guard at the entrance to a magical maze that Jack (Colin Ford), his female cohort Jillian (Chloe Grace Moretz), and a goose (Gilbert Gottfried) must make their way through. Chevy's character operates according to the rules of "Opposites Day," which means everything he says is a lie. While the movie itself is pretty dopey, his big scene is actually quite humorous. Chevy has fun saying one thing and letting his body language indicate the exact opposite.

Not Another Not Another Movie (2011) – A spoof of movie studios made by people who have absolutely no idea how movie studios work. Chevy plays Max Storm, head of the failing Sunshine Studios. After an especially big flop, he turns control over to his brother Lester (Michael Madsen). Chevy only has a few minutes of screen time in this achingly amateurish film. The bulk of the plot involves a production assistant (played by David Leo Schultz, who also "co-wrote" the "screenplay") who fails upward within the studio. A multitude of limp, unimaginative spoofs of various Hollywood blockbusters are scattered throughout. Chevy's big joke is that Max Storm earned his riches by opening an ice cream store that sold thirty flavors, then went out of business when Baskin-Robbins opened one that sold thirty-one. It is unknown what led Chevy (or Madsen, or Burt Reynolds, who also cameos) to appear in such dreck. Most likely, he needed a paycheck. Whatever the reason, seeing him surrounded by so many unfunny co-stars and delivering unfunny dialogue is depressing.

Conclusions

During the years 2006 to 2013, Chevy returned to the medium that made him famous: television. There was a cameo on *Law & Order*, brief runs on *Brothers & Sisters* and *Chuck*, and voice work in an episode of *Family Guy*. Then, in 2009. he scored what would be his most significant role in years, playing the aging hippie Pierce Hawthorne in the NBC comedy series *Community*.

Although not a big ratings hit, *Community* quickly developed a devoted cult following. It is nominally the story of a disgraced lawyer, played by Joel McHale, who hesitantly attends Greendale Community College to get the degree he only pretended to have. There, he falls in with an eccentric collection of fellow students in a study group, including the aforementioned Pierce.

Marked by hip, often meta humor, *Community* initially made wise use of Chevy's skills. Perhaps the most subtle joke of the show was that the man who once represented cutting edge comedy was now cast as a clueless old man, unable to keep up with the pop cultural references of his much younger cohorts. Chevy seemed to get the joke. For the first time in years, he'd found a role that really connected with the public – or at least the small-but-influential demographic that watched *Community*.

The good times did not last. The writers, apparently looking for more ways to show Pierce's antiquated world view, tossed in a few politically incorrect lines for him to utter. Rather than getting mileage from this joke and then letting it pass, Pierce ended up morphing into a full-fledged racist. This understandably displeased Chevy, who went on to engage in a series of very contentious public disputes with showrunner Dan Harmon. The entertainment news media had a field day reporting on the Chevy/Harmon squabbles, especially once Harmon publicly played a profanity-laden voice mail message Chevy left for him. (In Chevy's defense, it was in response to Harmon leading the *Community* crew in shouting "Fuck you, Chevy" to the actor during a wrap party at which his wife and daughter were present.) Harmon was fired from the show after the third season, but new showrunners David Guarascio and Moses Port kept Pierce Hawthore a racist. In some episodes, literally half the character's lines of dialogue were prejudiced nonsense. Chevy grew even more displeased, eventually leaving the show before its fourth season was completed.

If media reports are to be believed, there was a fair amount of bad behavior on both sides of the coin. Still, it's difficult not to empathize with Chevy's point of view. He's a comedian. He wants to be funny on screen. Racism is not funny. No comedian wants to be the person tasked with trying to make it funny.

Community didn't end happily for Chevy, but if nothing else, it proved that he still had the ability to connect with audiences, to be part of something that hit the mark. And until Pierce became an unrepentant bigot, Chevy delivered an enthusiastic performance, often earning the biggest laughs of the show. In spite of a career that had its share of ups and downs, he was clearly still in command of his comic gift.

And what a unique comic gift it is. In watching all of Chevy's movies over the course of a year, there are a number of conclusions that can safely be drawn:

Chevy's best movies were often book or article adaptations: *Fletch, Funny Farm, Memoirs of an Invisible Man, National Lampoon's Vacation* (based on John Hughes' "Vacation '58"). We'll just conveniently forget about *Zoom*.

Chevy worked with some A-list talent: His directors include Michael Ritchie, John Landis, George Roy Hill, Harold Ramis, Stephen Frears, John Carpenter, and William Friedkin. That's a list any working actor would kill to have. Chevy has also shared the screen with an impressive array of co-stars, including Steve Martin, Dustin Hoffman, Sigourney Weaver, Naomi Watts, Goldie Hawn, Rodney Dangerfield, Bill Murray, Dan Aykroyd, John Candy, Daryl Hannah, Jack Palance, and John Cusack, among many others.

"Hand Comedy" is prevalent in his work: Most of his movies have at least one scene in which Chevy uses his hands for comedy. In *Seems Like Old Times,* he hides under a bed and tries to signal Goldie Hawn with one hand that Charles Grodin is stepping on his other hand. In *Vegas Vacation,* he moves down a hideous looking buffet, fondling the disgusting food. In *Christmas Vacation,* he gets the pages of a magazine stuck on his sap-covered fingers. And let's not forget the "sex fingers" in *The Groove Tube.* Look closely in his movies and you'll find plenty more examples.

He's not afraid of repetition: Chevy played Clark Griswold four times, Fletch two times, and Ty Webb two times. He has twice played a high school principal (*Orange County* and *Stay Cool*) and twice done the voice of a dog trying to solve a murder (*Oh! Heavenly Dog* and *Karate Dog*). He also occasionally reuses jokes. In several of his pictures, including *Zoom* and *Caddyshack II,* he exits a scene by looking at his arm (which may or may not be sporting a watch) and declares, "I've got a thing."

A recurring theme in his movies is searching for perfection and not being able to find it: This theme drove *Vacation* and its sequels, as well as *Funny Farm*. Traces of it can also be found in *Memoirs of an Invisible Man* (narcissistic playboy wants to finally settle down with new love interest, only to have invisibility get in the way), *Man of the House* (guy wants to create a new family with his girlfriend, only to find her son resistant to his presence in the home), and *Cops and Robbersons* (guy wants his family to get along, only to have them fight more once a cop moves in).

Whenever he tried to stretch, it didn't work out, unlike many of his peers: Bill Murray found acceptance as a dramatic actor with *Lost in Translation* and *Broken Flowers*, among others. Dan Aykroyd got an Oscar nomination for *Driving Miss Daisy*. Steve Martin proved all-around renaissance man, giving acclaimed performances in both comedic (*Planes, Trains & Automobiles, Bowfinger, Parenthood*) and dramatic (*The Spanish Prisoner, Grand Canyon*) roles, authoring best-selling novels (*Shopgirl, The Pleasure of My Company*), writing plays, and recording bluegrass albums. Like his counterparts, Chevy tried to stretch and do things outside his wheelhouse. *Deal of the Century* was an edgier role. *Funny Farm* was a screwball comedy in classic style. *Memoirs of an Invisible Man* was a character-based special effects thriller. He even took supporting roles in ambitious projects like *Hero,* wherein he could work alongside A+ talent on both sides of the camera. Every time he stretched, though, things didn't seem to click. Either audiences rejected the effort (as with *Memoirs* and *Funny Farm*), or the movie's reach exceeded its grasp (as with *Deal* and *Hero*). Other times, he gave nuanced performances in movies where everything else failed to match his commitment (*Man of the House, Funny Money*). One of his finest, and most atypical, turns came in *Ellie Parker*, a small indie that few people saw. Taking these things into consideration, it should be firmly understood that a frequent criticism of Chevy – that he has a small repertoire – is patently untrue. Closer inspection of his filmography reveals that he did, in fact, take chances. He delivered work that was of a high caliber, both comedically and dramatically. Likely due to the fact that his bombs were so high-profile (*Oh! Heavenly Dog, Nothing but Trouble, Under the Rainbow*), the stuff that didn't work tended to overshadow the times where Chevy really ventured outside the box.

As of this writing in late spring 2013, Chevy has several projects on the way, according to IMDb. One is a drama called *Before I Sleep,* the other a comedy entitled *Lovesick.* Both appear to be independent productions. He has also signed on to reprise his role as Repairman in *Hot Tub Time Machine 2.* A new *Vacation* is also in development at New Line Pictures. The plot reportedly centers around the now-grown Rusty trying to take his own family on a trip. Chevy and Beverly D'Angelo are expected to cameo, should the film actually get made. As of press time, it had been delayed due to "creative differences" between the studio, which wants a PG-13 comedy, and the filmmakers, who want something more R-rated.

Chevy Chase has made classics and turkeys, major Hollywood productions and tiny independent efforts. He has taken lead roles and supporting parts. He has co-starred with some of the most talented people in the business and performed under the guidance of Oscar-winning directors. He's given audiences the crazy comedy they love, while also occasionally veering outside his comfort zone. Most importantly, he's provided a lot of laughter to a lot of people. No matter how you cut it, he has made his mark in the world of screen comedy. Thanks to the enduring popularity of, in particular, *Caddyshack, Fletch,* and the *Vacation* series, his legacy is likely to endure for generations to come.

Chevy Chase *is* the ball. *Na na na na na...*

About the Author

Mike McGranaghan is the film critic for The Aisle Seat website (AisleSeat.com) and the radio stations of Sunbury Broadcasting Corporation. He was a regular contributor to Current TV's movie review program, "The Rotten Tomatoes Show." Mike is a member of the Online Film Critics Society, as well as the winner of a Pennsylvania Association of Broadcasters award. His work has been published in *Paracinema* magazine and online at Film Racket. Mike's first book, a collection of movie-related essays entitled *Straight-Up Blatant: Musings From The Aisle Seat*, is available in paperback and Kindle editions. He lives in Central Pennsylvania with his wife and son.

Follow Mike McGranaghan on Twitter: @aisleseat

About the Illustrator

Mike Bennett is a talented artist and podcaster extraordinaire. He is the proprietor of Mike Bennett Illustration (Facebook.com/MikeBennettIllustration). Mike is also one of the hosts of the very successful *Popular Outcasts* podcast, which you can – and should - listen to at PopularOutcasts.net or on iTunes.

Follow Mike Bennett on Twitter: @two2tone22

25705880R00070

Printed in Great Britain
by Amazon